Surviving *Padilla*

A Defender's Guide to Advising Noncitizens on the Immigration Consequences of Criminal Convictions

Kara Hartzler
Florence Immigrant and Refugee Rights Project

Florence, Arizona, USA

ISBN 978-1-257-71527-5

Printed in the United States of America.

About the Author

Kara Hartzler is the Legal Director and Criminal Immigration Consultant at the Florence Immigrant and Refugee Rights Project. Since 2007, she has headed the Arizona Defending Immigrants Partnership and provided over 3,000 advisals to defendants and their attorneys on the immigration consequences of criminal convictions. She teaches a course on Immigration and Crimes at the University of Arizona James E. Rogers College of Law and regularly appears before the immigration court, the Board of Immigration Appeals, the U.S. District Court of Arizona, and the Ninth Circuit Court of Appeals. In 2010, Ms. Hartzler received the Robert J. Hooker Award from the Arizona Public Defender Association, which recognizes a private attorney who has provided extraordinary assistance to public defenders. She lives with her husband and dog in Oracle, Arizona.

Acknowledgements

I am deeply grateful to Laura Belous, Tally Kingsnorth, Lindsay Marshall, and Ryan Moore for their insightful comments and critical feedback on this book. Thanks also to Jack Chin for writing the introduction and his extensive work on *Padilla.*

The Arizona defense bar has patiently educated me on criminal law and procedure and has truly shaped my work in this field. In particular, I am grateful to all the public defenders who have inspired me with their passion for indigent defense and their daily struggle for constitutional rights and civil liberties.

The Florence Project has been my home for six years, and my colleagues past and present are some of the most dedicated, intelligent, and compassionate people I have known. They drive out into the middle of the desert every day to do high-stakes, heartbreaking work and somehow manage to keep a wicked sense of humor. They are my friends and my inspiration and I consider myself a success when I live up to their standards.

I have been lucky to have the support and mentorship of members of the national Defending Immigrants Partnership, as well as the sage wisdom of my parents on the business of books, marketing, and life.

Most of all, thanks to Sébastien, who tolerated my daily five a.m. writing sessions, kept the formatting wolves at bay, and supported me unconditionally throughout this process.

Kara Hartzler

Contents

Introduction: Making *Padilla* Practical and Possible

by Professor Gabriel "Jack" Chin
University of California, Davis School of Law

Civil attorneys recognize that client matters do not arrive in the office pre-labeled as "Tort" or "Contract" issues. Therefore, a competent civil attorney dealing with almost any situation--a securities fraud case, a medical malpractice suit, negotiating an employment contract or drafting an estate plan--will, routinely, almost instinctively, consider contract and tort aspects of the problem, tax, regulatory and administrative implications, and even the possibility of criminal liability of their client or adversary. Good lawyers recognize that cases should be analyzed, not pigeonholed.

Civil attorneys also pay close attention to the collateral estoppel and res judicata implications of their decisions. A claim not raised in this lawsuit will be barred forever; losing this little lawsuit may mean that the facts are established by collateral estoppel for one with a thousand times more at stake.

By contrast, in criminal cases, many courts have held that the defense attorney's responsibility is much more limited. Instead of advancing the client's legal interests generally, rather than considering the possible effects of this plea in other cases, the attorney is expected to look solely at the criminal consequences, and solely at the particular case at issue. Thus, over the years thousands of clients have pleaded guilty to crimes and received what appeared to be fine deals—probation, time served—until they learned for the first time what neither their lawyer nor the court ever told them: That their plea means they will be deported, or lose their ability to earn a living, or be kicked out of public housing, or lose custody of a child. Catastrophic results from lawyers' advice, courts said, was entirely consistent with due process and the right to counsel.

Astonishingly, courts even held that advice to plead guilty to one charge when already facing a capital charge was perfectly acceptable, without warning that taking the plea would mean that it was more likely that the client would be sentenced to death and executed. *See Ex parte* Morrow, 952 S.W.2d 530, 535 (Tex. Crim. App. 1997)). As Judge Danny Boggs of the Sixth Circuit explained, execution "is only a collateral consequence of his guilty plea, and [the defendant's] ignorance of the possible consequence does not render his plea involuntary." King v. Dutton, 17 F.3d 151, 154 (6th Cir. 1994).

This inexcusably narrow vision of lawyering was exploded in 2010 in *Padilla v. Kentucky*, where seven justices held that important consequences like deportation flowing automatically from the criminal conviction were part of defense counsel's responsibility under the Sixth Amendment.

For some attorneys, *Padilla* changed nothing; they were already considering deportation and other collateral consequences as part of representation. But as the norms of criminal practice borrow something from civil lawyers, it must be recognized that there is a major difference: Most civil clients are paying, most clients of defense lawyers are indigent. In a civil case, if a tax issue arises, perhaps there is a tax department at the firm, or the client is going to have to come up with the money to hire a tax lawyer. Indigent defendants simply do not have money to hire specialized counsel. In an ideal world of unlimited resources, it would be wonderful to spend $10,000 in every case involving a client who might be a noncitizen to do an exhaustive, gold-plated immigration work-up. But in the real world, the only thing a client has, the client's only hope, is their criminal defense attorney, and the efforts he or she is willing to make on their behalf to get the best outcome.

That's where this expert and useful book comes in. *Padilla* means that public defenders and assigned counsel are expected to become reasonably competent in a new area of civil law. Spending several hours reading this book will not turn a criminal defense attorney into a full-fledged immigration expert. However, it will give any lawyer a functional, working understanding of the issues, a method for analyzing criminal cases involving noncitizens, and a set of strategies and techniques to get the best outcome for the client. This book will enable defense counsel to give solid advice in most cases, and how to figure out when more expert help is necessary. The book also gives attorneys practical and informed advice about dealing with every relevant constituency: prosecutors, immigration attorneys, federal authorities, and the client him or herself.

Some of the book's advice will be counter-intuitive: Sometimes it is better for the client to be convicted of a higher offense, rather than a lesser, or to serve more time, rather than less. But attorneys making an effort to understand the immigration implications and their client's choices, will find tools to get better outcomes, and to serve the overall interests of their clients. Most people going into criminal defense work do so in large part to help their clients. This book will help them do it.

Professor Chin was co-author of the ABA Amicus Brief in Padilla v. Kentucky, *and of* Effective Assistance of Counsel and the Collateral Consequences of Guilty Pleas, *87 Cornell L. Rev. 697 (2002), cited in the majority and concurring opinions.*

INTRODUCTION

OUTLINE OF "THE ADVISAL"

Step 1: Inadmissible or Deportable?

INADMISSIBLE

- Undocumented
- Lawful Permanent Resident (LPR) at border or airport
- "Work permit"
- Person "paroled" into U.S.

DEPORTABLE

- Visa/Border Crossing Card
- Lawful Permanent Resident (LPR) inside the U.S.
- I-94
- Passport stamp

Step 2: Applicable Grounds of Removal

Criminal Grounds of Inadmissibility

- Crime involving moral turpitude (CIMT)
- Controlled substance
- Reason to believe drug trafficker
- Reason to believe trafficker in persons
- Prostitution
- False claim to U.S. citizenship
- Encouraged/assisted another alien to enter U.S. illegally

Criminal Grounds of Deportability

- Crime involving moral turpitude (CIMT) within five years of admission
- 2 CIMTs at any time
- Aggravated felony
- Controlled substance (exception for 30 grams or less of marijuana)
- Firearms
- Domestic violence, stalking, or child abuse
- Violation of a protection order
- False claim to U.S. citizenship
- Encouraged/assisted another alien to enter U.S. illegally

Most Common Aggravated Felonies

- Murder, rape, sexual abuse of a minor
- Drug trafficking
- Certain firearms/explosives offenses
- Crime of violence ≥ 1 year actual sentence
- Theft/Burglary/Receiving Stolen Property ≥ 1 year actual sentence
- Fraud/Money Laundering with loss of more than $10K to victim
- Forgery/Counterfeiting ≥ 1 year actual sentence
- Obstruction of justice ≥ 1 year actual sentence
- Running a Prostitution Business
- Alien Smuggling under 8 U.S.C. § 1324
- Failure to Appear (for offense with 2 or 5 year sentence)
- Attempt or Conspiracy to commit any of above

Step 3: Categorical Match?

1. Consult state-specific immigration chart
2. Compare plain language of immigration ground and state statute
3. Refer to descriptions of grounds in Step Two
4. Research immigration sourcebooks
5. Search Lexis or Westlaw for key terms
6. Search cases in annotated state code

Travel outside U.S. and circuit

Relief from Removal

- Voluntary departure
- Cancellation of Removal for Permanent and Nonpermanent Residents
- Asylum, withholding of removal, Convention Against Torture
- Adjustment and Readjustment of Status
- Victim of domestic violence from U.S. citizen or LPR
- S, T, or U visa
- Special visa for juveniles who've been abused, abandoned, or neglected
- Temporary Protected Status (TPS)
- Claim to automatically acquired or derived U.S. citizenship
- NACARA

Immigration Bonds

Part I:

Getting Started

Chapter One:
WHO SHOULD USE THIS BOOK?

Chapter Two:
WHAT DOES *PADILLA* REQUIRE?

Chapter Three:
WHAT INFORMATION DO I NEED?

Chapter One:

Who Should Use This Book?

This book is for the criminal defense attorney who's exhausted and overwhelmed and wishes he didn't have to worry about immigration consequences. It's for the public defender sitting on the subway, balancing a muffin and coffee, desperately trying to figure out whether her client is going to be deported for the plea that he's scheduled to accept in a few hours. It's for the defender who is deeply committed to providing the best possible representation for his clients but has no interest in becoming an immigration lawyer.

Since the U.S. Supreme Court issued its landmark Sixth Amendment decision in *Padilla v. Kentucky* on March 31, 2010, defenders across the country have been scrambling to find a consistent, affordable, and feasible way to advise their clients on the immigration consequences of criminal convictions. But while there are many resources available on the *substance* of immigration law, few focus on *how to use* that information to provide the actual advisal.

The purpose of this book is to teach defense attorneys a practical method of complying with *Padilla* that won't overwhelm their limited resources. Since 2007, I've worked closely with defense attorneys to provide over 3,000 advisals to their clients on the immigration consequences of criminal convictions. This book represents the formula I've developed after much trial and error to explain immigration law to defenders in a way that doesn't make them want to flee or curl up in the fetal position. It avoids any citations, footnotes, and endnotes that aren't absolutely necessary and echews the typical language of a legal treatise in favor of a straightforward "how to" approach.

The core of this book is a three step framework for determining the immigration consequences of a particular criminal conviction. While it can't answer every question about every case, it's designed to teach you how to give advice on the majority of offenses for the majority of clients you encounter. The book also gives practical tips on explaining these issues to your client, advising on important corollary issues such as travel and relief from removal, negotiating with unsympathetic prosecutors, and avoiding the most common mistakes on immigration issues.

Padilla isn't going away, and the days in which a defense attorney could remain blissfully ignorant of immigration law have passed. I've met defense attorneys who continue to resist this and will only be led down the immigration path kicking and screaming. But the majority of defenders, albeit with considerable trepidation, are willing to wade into this area if they can find an accessible and easy to understand way to do it. They want to comply with their Sixth Amendment obligations, but even more so, they care about their clients and want to do the best they can to defend their interests. This book is designed for those defenders – to try to make the learning curve as horizontal as possible, to provide an accessible porthole in immigration law, and to do so without increasing their level of anxiety.

Step back from the ledge. It's going to be OK.

<u>Chapter Two:</u>

WHAT DOES *PADILLA* REQUIRE?

In this chapter:

- Overview of the *Padilla* decision
- Three interpretations of the *Padilla* advisal

Before we can talk about *how* to advise clients on the immigration consequences of criminal convictions, we have to decide the *scope* of the advice we'll be giving. So let's start with the decision itself.

Overview of the Padilla *Decision*

In *Padilla v. Kentucky,* 130 S.Ct. 1473 (2010), the Supreme Court considered the case of a longtime lawful permanent resident who pleaded guilty to a drug trafficking offense in reliance on his criminal defense attorney's statement that he would not be deported. After realizing this advice was incorrect, Mr. Padilla sought to vacate his conviction based on his Sixth Amendment right to effective assistance of counsel.

The majority held that, not only was the performance of Mr. Padilla's counsel ineffective, but that failure to affirmatively advise a client on the immigration consequences of a plea falls below the standard of a reasonable attorney – in other words, silence is not sufficient. The court acknowledged the complexity of immigration law but concluded that when the immigration consequences of a plea are "truly clear," a defense attorney must advise her client of these consequences. When the consequences are unclear, the attorney must at least warn the client that a risk of deportation exists.

Since *Padilla* was issued, a variety of interpretations have emerged regarding what kind of advisal the decision actually requires. Here are the most common:

The "One-Size-Fits-All" Advisal

Some practitioners contend that a defender's requirements under *Padilla* can be satisfied by an identical warning, given to all non-U.S. citizen clients, that "there may be immigration consequences if you take this plea." Whether it's a generic warning provided by the judge, a clause in the plea agreement, a one-sentence advisal given by the defense attorney, or a warning to talk to an immigration lawyer, all that's required is to advise defendants that a risk of deportation exists and *Padilla* has been satisfied.

The problem with this generic advisal is that it's fundamentally incompatible with the language of *Padilla*. *Padilla* requires that defenders inform the client when consequences are "truly clear" and when they aren't. Furthermore, *Padilla* noted that, at a minimum, the defense attorney could have reviewed the grounds of deportability and discovered that Mr. Padilla's offense fell squarely within one. In other words, a simple recitation to all noncitizens that this plea "could have immigration consequences" or that the defendant "should talk to an immigration lawyer" will fall short of the requirement that the defense attorney must advise the client on the *specific* consequences of the plea for the client's *individual* situation.

Furthermore, *Padilla* is a Sixth Amendment case, which provides for a right to effective *counsel*. A judge or a written plea agreement is not a defendant's lawyer and cannot assume a lawyer's duties. While a generic advisal at the time of sentencing or a line in a plea agreement may be required by a particular court's rules of criminal procedure, such advisals do not distinguish between when deportation is "truly clear," and when there is merely a "risk" of it, as *Padilla* mandates.

In fact, there are situations in which a One-Size-Fits-All Advisal could arguably constitute *affirmative misadvice*. Consider a client who's been offered a plea to an offense that would *not* cause deportation. The defense attorney gives the client a generic advisal that "there's a risk of deportation if you take this plea" and the client, terrified at the prospect of being deported, decides to go to trial. The client loses at trial and has now been convicted of an offense that *will* cause deportation. Did the defender's warning of a "risk of deportation," when none actually existed, constitute affirmative misadvice and create prejudice?

I understand the reluctance to place this burden on already overwhelmed defenders, the desire to prevent a flood of ineffective assistance claims, the concern about whether this holding applies to hundreds of other collateral consequences, and the fear of how *Padilla* could fundamentally alter the nature of the criminal justice system. But the bottom line is that the One-Size-Fits-All Advisal theory is not supported by, and cannot be reconciled with, the language of *Padilla*. Period.

The "Perfect" Advisal

Some judges, defenders, and immigration attorneys have greeted *Padilla* with all the enthusiasm of a messianic promise fulfilled. "Finally," they say, "noncitizens can always know *exactly* how a plea will affect their immigration status."

I hate to take a razor blade to this bubble. But anyone who tells you that he can always predict the exact immigration consequences of every criminal plea is grossly unfamiliar with the immigration system. Here's why:

Immigration case law is unsettled.

At its core, predicting immigration consequences requires the application of numerous "generic definitions" listed in the federal immigration statute (e.g., "aggravated felony," "crime involving moral turpitude," "burglary") to the statutes of fifty different states and countless municipalities. These federal generic definitions are terms of art, and you can't necessarily tell at first glance whether they will match the elements of a particular state or local statute. So in most situations, we look to case law that addressed similar statutes from other jurisdictions and try to use those decisions to guess whether our own state statute would meet the federal definition. At best, it's a highly educated prediction. At worst, it's a shot in the dark.

Immigration judges can reasonably disagree.

When you have hundreds of immigration judges (not to mention thousands of agency adjudicators) all deciding whether Statute X is a "crime involving moral turpitude" with no settled case law to guide them, consistency is a huge problem. It is not unusual for Judge A to hold that Statute X is a CIMT while Judge B holds the opposite. Because there's no way to predict whether a person will be assigned to Judge A or Judge B, you can't always advise your client on the exact immigration consequences.

Clients are transferred to different jurisdictions.

Immigration detention has tripled in the last fifteen years, with the majority of beds concentrated in remote areas along the southern border. Meanwhile, circuit courts of appeal, which create a huge body of law on immigration issues, reach different conclusions on the same legal questions. As a result, it's not unusual to plead your client to an offense that is not deportable, only to have her transferred to a circuit where it *is* deportable. So unless you've researched the law of all eleven circuits, you can't know the immigration consequences with certainty.

You may be wallowing in despair at this moment, wondering how Justice Stevens could be so cruel as to require you to do an impossible advisal on an area of law for which you never signed up. But there's one more interpretation of *Padilla* left, and – you guessed it – it's the one described in this book.

The "Realistic" Advisal

Somewhere between the One-Size-Fits-All Advisal and the Perfect Advisal, there's a way to alert your clients to the immigration consequences of a conviction that will allow them to make a knowing and voluntary plea. As with any other area of law, an attorney can never predict the exact outcome with one hundred percent accuracy. But we can use the resources available to us to suggest the probable outcome of a given set of circumstances. That's what this book is designed to teach you.

Some advocates contend that defense attorneys with no experience in immigration law have no business advising on immigration consequences. They argue that in each and every case involving a noncitizen defendant, an immigration expert should prepare a detailed memorandum on the exact immigration consequences of the conviction that is meticulously reviewed with the client prior to accepting the plea.

I like this idea a lot. But the last time I checked, most public defender offices and private practices were being slashed to the bone and have no realistic way of paying a consultation fee to an expert immigration lawyer in every case where a noncitizen is facing criminal charges. So for the moment, a perfect system in which every noncitizen receives a consultation with an expert immigration attorney is going to remain a pleasant fantasy.

When it comes to *Padilla*, the perfect should not be the enemy of the good. The fact that a defense lawyer cannot predict immigration consequences with absolute certainty doesn't mean he has to resort to giving a vague one-size-fits-all advisal for every noncitizen client. Like every other area of law, we investigate our client's situation, we research the applicable authority, and then we do the best we can to give our clients a cautious yet realistic assessment of the consequences. The trick is knowing what this is and how to explain it to your client. So let's get started.

Summary of important points:

- *Padilla* found that defense attorneys have an affirmative duty to advise their noncitizen clients on immigration consequences. Silence is not sufficient.
- When the immigration consequences of a plea are "truly clear," the defender must advise the client of this. When the immigration consequences are unclear, the defender must, at a minimum, advise that a risk of deportation exists.
- A generic advisal given to all that noncitizens that a plea "may lead to deportation" is not sufficient to satisfy *Padilla.*

Chapter Three:

WHAT INFORMATION DO I NEED?

In this chapter:

- Critical questions to ask the client
- Knowing when you're in over your head
- Client priorities
- Working with immigration attorneys

The next step is figuring out the information we'll need. At this stage, it's also helpful to consider how important immigration consequences are to the client and to identify the situations where you'll need to consult an expert. Finally, if the client already has an immigration attorney, you'll need to consult with her and navigate the issues that can arise from working with a client's immigration lawyer.

What Questions Should I Ask the Client?

Before you can even think of advising a client on immigration consequences, you have to ask him some key questions. It's helpful to have as detailed a picture as possible of the client's situation, so later I'll list other information that you should gather. But if you're in a pressure situation, this is the absolute minimum you must have in order to advise a client on immigration consequences:

The Five Absolutely Critical Questions

1. **When did you last enter the U.S.?**
2. **How did you enter? (e.g. illegally, visa, "green card," parole)**
3. **Did you ever get a green card, visa, or other legal permission to be here? If so, when did you get it?**
4. **Have you ever been deported or put into deportation proceedings?**
5. **What priors do you have? (including misdemeanors)**

Why do you need to know this information? Here's a breakdown of each question:

1. **"When did you last enter the U.S.?"**

   Some grounds of deportation will be triggered based on the timing of the offense, the most common being the commission of a "crime involving moral turpitude" (CIMT) within five years of being legally admitted to the U.S. Also, some clients, even if they can be removed, may be eligible for a waiver to stay in the U.S. depending on when they entered.

2. **"How did you enter?" (e.g. illegally, visa, "green card," parole)**

   This is a critical question since it provides essential information about which set of legal grounds will control the client's removal. The two common answers will be, "I came through the desert/river/border without papers," and "I came through a border or airport with my visa/green card/other document."

   When asking this question, it's also important to identify whether the client was taken into custody at a border port-of-entry or airport (even temporarily). Even if the client is allowed to enter the U.S. and is not in custody during any subsequent proceeding, the fact that the client was entering the U.S. at the time she was identified by immigration will subject her to a different set of laws that will affect removability, bond, and eligibility to apply for a waiver.

3. **"Did you ever get a green card, visa, or other legal permission to be here? If so, when did you get it?"**

   While the first two questions focused on the *manner of entry*, this question is designed to elicit information on the client's *current immigration status*, which may have changed since the client first entered. For instance, even if a client entered illegally, he may have subsequently obtained lawful permanent residence through family or an employer, which will change the applicable laws.

   Keep an eye out for quirky exceptions:

   There's a few situations that come up repeatedly and may confuse you as to whether a person has current lawful status:

   - **The "10-year visa" (also known as a "laser visa" or "border crossing card")**

     Many immigrants along the border have a multiple-entry visa that is valid for ten years but only allows them to come to the U.S. for work or travel for a maximum of six months at a time. If a client tells you he's been here legally for two years on a visitor's visa and it's good for another eight years, he probably overstayed his visa and does not have current lawful status.

- **"Amnesty" with no green card**

  In the late 1980's, many noncitizens received "amnesty" as a Special Agricultural Worker (SAW) and went on to obtain permanent residence. However, if a client tells you he got "amnesty," make sure to ask if he later received a green card. If he didn't, Immigration and Customs Enforcement (ICE) may charge him as being undocumented.

- **"Parole"**

  In most cases, a noncitizen who passes through a border or airport has been legally admitted to the U.S. But in some cases, a person is "paroled" into the U.S. at a port-of-entry for certain compelling humanitarian reasons, to serve as a material witness, or to undergo criminal prosecution. If a person is "paroled" into the U.S., she is legally treated as though she is still at the border even though she has been allowed to physically enter the U.S.

- **"Work permit"**

  Many people enter the U.S. on valid work *visas* and, as such, have been legally "admitted" to the U.S. Many others entered illegally but have since been issued a valid work *permit,* also known as an Employment Authorization Document (EAD), as a result of a petition filed by a family member, an application for relief from removal, or a type of temporary status that allows them to live and work in the U.S. However, the issuance of an EAD does not, by itself, constitute a legal admission or valid immigration status. If a client tells you she has a "work permit," ask whether it's a visa that she used to enter or whether she received it after entering as a result of another process.

4. "Have you ever been deported or put into deportation proceedings?"

A client may be ineligible to receive legal status for ten years if she has previous immigration violations, such as a deportation, an illegal reentry after a deportation, or an illegal reentry after having been unlawfully present in the U.S. for more than a year. If the client is already ineligible to obtain legal status for the foreseeable future, the immigration consequences of a plea may be less important to her. Also, some clients receive waivers for criminal convictions that are only available once, so it's important to know whether your client may have already been granted a waiver in a removal hearing.

5. "What priors do you have? (including misdemeanors)"

An absolutely essential question. If the client already has an offense that makes him removable or prevents him from getting legal status in the future, the immigration consequences of the current plea may be irrelevant. Also, the existence of a prior conviction – even a misdemeanor – may change the outcome of the current plea.

Other Strongly Recommended Questions

These five questions are the absolute minimum that must be asked in order to advise a client on the immigration consequences of a plea. However, there are other questions that are strongly recommended in order to have a more complete picture of the client's immigration situations. I've listed these questions here and explained in parentheses why this information could be relevant.

- Were any of your parents or grandparents born in the U.S.? (potential citizenship claim)
- Did you have a green card and did one or both of your parents naturalize before you turned 18? (potential citizenship claim)
- Has anyone in your family ever submitted a petition for you or one of your parents? (eligible for a green card)
- Did you enter legally and:
    1) you are married to a U.S. citizen;
    2) you are under 21 and the child of a U.S. citizen; or
    3) you are the parent of a U.S. citizen child who is 21 or older? (immediately eligible for a green card)
- Do you have a U.S. citizen or permanent resident spouse, child, or parent who suffers from a medical or psychological condition? (helpful in applying for a waiver)
- If you were deported, do you think someone might harm you because of your race, religion, nationality, political opinion or membership in a particular social group? (asylum-based protections)
- If you were deported, do you think you would be tortured or killed? (protection under the Convention Against Torture)

- If still a minor, have you been declared dependent on the state, or have you been abused, abandoned, or neglected? (eligible for a green card)
- Have you ever:
  1) been the victim of a crime and been helpful or willing to be helpful to law enforcement; (eligible for visa)
  2) been the victim of trafficking and been helpful or willing to be helpful to law enforcement; (eligible for visa)
  3) had important information about high-level criminal activity (such as drug or human smuggling) that you'd be willing to share with law enforcement? (eligible for visa)
- Do you have an immigration lawyer? (if so, contact immediately)

There will always be other relevant questions, but the answers to these will give you a strong indication of the client's current immigration status and potential for relief.

What If the Client Doesn't Care About Immigration Consequences?

There will be situations in which a client tells you, "I don't care about immigration, just get me out of here as quickly as possible!" Does such a statement absolve a defense attorney of her responsibilities under *Padilla*?

The reality, as we all know, is that many clients are frustrated and scared such that they bellow and bluster a lot of things they don't mean. But others are expressing perfectly rational sentiments about their defense priorities. How can we tell the difference?

This will always be a judgment call, and as such, I would err on the side of caution. The thing about immigration is that it's *forever*. Clients who are incarcerated can't always see beyond the next few days or weeks, and they will swear they are NEVER coming back to the U.S. But in a few years when Mom turns eighty or Little Susie is forgetting the sound of Dad's voice, even the most adamant client may consult an immigration lawyer to see whether there's a chance of returning legally to the U.S. When that happens, the lawyer will need a legal hook to reopen the case and they'll come looking at – yup, whether you provided ineffective assistance under *Padilla*.

There will also be clients who say, "No, my whole family is in _____, I own a house there, I just want to take the deal that will get me back as quickly as possible."

There's nothing inherently wrong with this as long as you think the client is judging the situation objectively. For instance, if the client has four U.S. citizen children and tells you to take the plea that will most quickly get him deported, ask: "So are your kids going to move to Mexico with you?" Push him to imagine what his life will look like in five, ten, or twenty years if he's living outside the U.S. Many clients believe that even if they get deported this time, they can just apply through a relative and come back legally in the future. But if a client has legal status and is being deported on account of a criminal conviction, this same conviction will usually prevent the client from returning to the U.S. again, even on a visa.

Even if a client claims not to care about immigration consequences, keep in mind that he may be considering whether to illegally reenter in the future. If he does, his criminal history can be used as a sentencing enhancement for a federal illegal reentry charge, resulting in sentences of up to twenty years. Federal defenders (and their clients) would greatly appreciate it if you warn your client about this.

How Do I Know When I'm In Over My Head?

This guide is designed to assist defense attorneys in the majority of straightforward immigration cases. But as in every area of law, it's important to know your limits and recognize when a case is too complicated to handle on your own. Here are a few signs that you need to consult an expert:

- **You can't figure out the client's immigration status.**

  Immigration law contains a myriad of quirky types of status, and there will always be times when your client says vaguely that she has some sort of permission to be in the U.S. but she can't tell you what it is. These situations are particularly vulnerable to the consequences of criminal convictions, so if you can't figure out what type of immigration status you're working with, consult an expert.

- **You can't figure out the law in a high-stakes case.**

  Client has been in the U.S. legally for thirty years and has a kid with learning disabilities, a wife with depression, and a father with diabetes. He's repeatedly expressed to you that immigration consequences are his highest priority but you're having a hard time figuring out whether his conviction for insurance fraud will be deportable. Consult an immigration expert who practices in your georgraphical area – not only for the law, but to find out how local immigration judges would likely treat such a case.

What If the Client Already Has an Immigration Lawyer?

If the client tells you she has an immigration lawyer, it's extremely important to discuss any pleas with the attorney, even ones that won't result in deportation. In most immigration matters, attorneys are responsible to disclose *every* arrest and conviction, and a failure to do so could be fatal to the person's application for a visa, a green card, or naturalization.

However, working with an immigration lawyer can be tricky. Here are a few common issues that arise and how to handle them:

➢ **The Immigration Lawyer won't call me back.**

The single most common complaint I hear from defenders is that the immigration lawyer won't return phone calls or e-mails. I agree this is extremely frustrating since any good immigration lawyer, upon hearing that all their work could be undone by a single plea, should be on the phone to you in five minutes or less. Unless the lawyer is no longer representing the client, there's no excuse for an immigration attorney not to return your call.

However, this is an epidemic among lawyers in general, and there will always be cases where you just can't get your client's immigration attorney to return your calls. When this happens, make sure you've left at least three messages, and document when and where you left them. Then do your own analysis of the immigration consequences, and on the fourth message say, "I have done independent research and I believe that the best plea for immigration purposes is this. I've advised the client of the immigration consequences and she will be taking a plea to this on Monday morning unless I hear from you."

➢ **The Immigration Lawyer has unrealistic expectations.**

Another common frustration for defenders is when the client's immigration lawyer keeps pushing for a plea that no prosecutor would ever accept. "I know he's charged with importing two tons of marijuana," the attorney will chirp. "But can't you just plead him to a misdemeanor disorderly conduct?"

Remember that many immigration attorneys have no experience in criminal law and no idea of what a realistic plea would be. Furthermore, immigration attorneys are often under the impression that defenders can just make up any old plea language they want, not understanding that there really does have to be a legitimate connection between what happened and the factual basis for the offense.

Try to give the immigration attorney a brief explanation of what a prosecutor would usually accept in this situation. "Well, the client has been offered a plea to a felony, and I don't see any way a prosecutor will realistically accept a misdemeanor. Also, the client didn't do anything that would be considered disruptive or disorderly, so I can't make a factual basis for disorderly conduct. Here's what they're alleging the client did: if you can find a felony that fits that factual basis, I can definitely try to get the prosecutor to accept it."

Inevitably, there will be stand-offs. The immigration attorney has to have a certain plea in order for the client to stay in the U.S., but you know you can't get it. She may even accuse you of being difficult or not caring about the fact that the client will be deported. Take a deep breath and explain that you will not be able to get the plea she wants, but that if the client doesn't want to accept the plea, he can always go to trial. If that happens, your prediction is that the client will lose, so the immigration lawyer needs to either find a felony that fits the factual basis or deal with a client who's been convicted of importing two tons of marijuana.

In sum, you will always have immigration attorneys with unrealistic expectations. But rather than rejecting their suggestions with no explanation (which will only antagonize them), your best bet is to explain what kind of plea you can get, what kind of factual basis you're working with, and invite them to give you suggestions.

- **The Immigration Lawyer tries to communicate through the client.**

If you're playing phone tag or the immigration attorney isn't returning calls, it may be tempting to communicate about the specifics of a plea via the client. Don't. There's too much potential for misunderstanding, particularly when you're trying to relay legal jargon through a client who's easily confused. There's nothing wrong with having a three-way call or a conversation with both attorneys *and* the client, but don't ever use the client as your primary means of communication with the other attorney.

Conclusion

We've received the relevant information from the client and navigated a few preliminary hurdles. Now it's time to dive into the three step process.

Summary of important points:

- There are at least five critical questions you must ask the client in order to determine the immigration consequences of a plea:
  1. When did you last enter the U.S.?
  2. How did you enter? (e.g. illegally, visa, "green card," parole)
  3. Did you ever get a green card, visa, or other legal permission to be here? If so, when did you get it?
  4. Have you ever been deported or put into deportation proceedings?
  5. What priors do you have? (including misdemeanors)
- To be safe, give a *Padilla* advisal even if the client tells you he doesn't care about immigration consequences.
- Consult an immigration attorney if you can't figure out the client's status or the relevant law in a high-stakes case.
- Working with some immigration attorneys can be challenging; tell them what the prosecutor will accept and ask for suggestions.

Part II

THE THREE STEP PROCESS

<u>Chapter Four:</u>

OVERVIEW OF THE THREE STEP PROCESS

In this chapter:

- Explanation of the three step "IAC" advisal
- How often are immigration consequences "truly clear"?

Analyzing the immigration consequences of a plea for a noncitizen client is a three step process. First, you figure out which set of laws will apply to the client. Second, you review that set of laws to identify the potential grounds of removal. Third, you analyze whether the conviction will trigger one of those grounds of removal.

When I was explaining this three step process to my husband, he said, "So first you figure out their situation, then you think about all the things that COULD screw them up, then you find out whether those things will ACTUALLY screw them up." Exactly.

To help us remember those three steps, let's use a cheesy mnemonic device that sums up why we're all here: **IAC** (which usually stands for "ineffective assistance of counsel"). If you're representing a noncitizen and want to avoid an IAC claim, you'll need to figure out three questions:

(I)nadmissible or Deportable?

(A)pplicable Grounds of Removal?

(C)ategorical Match?

These phrases make no sense at this point, so here's an initial explanation of each one:

Inadmissible or Deportable?

If a noncitizen is convicted of a crime, he can be rendered either 1) ineligible to be admitted to the U.S. in the future or 2) currently deportable from the U.S. This is the step where you figure out the category into which your client falls. Why do we do this? Because the grounds of inadmissibility and deportability significantly differ, and a plea that makes a client inadmissible will not necessarily make a client deportable, and vice versa. Therefore, it's impossible to accurately determine the immigration consequences of a plea if we don't know which set of legal grounds will apply.

Applicable Grounds of Removal?

This is the step where we identify the potential grounds of inadmissibility or deportability that the plea might trigger. For instance, if the client is pleading to burglary, this conviction might be deportable as: 1) a crime involving moral turpitude; 2) an aggravated felony as a burglary/theft offense; and 3) an aggravated felony as a crime of violence. At this step, it's not necessary to reach a conclusion; we're only identifying the *potential* grounds that could be triggered.

Categorical Match?

This is the step where we analyze whether the plea will be an actual match to the identified ground of inadmissibility or deportability. In other words, we look at whether there are any differences between the elements of the state statute and the elements of immigration law such that the conviction will not automatically trigger removal. It's the most challenging and intimidating step, but we'll discuss a variety of resources that are available to help you in this process.

Example:

Say you've got a client who tells you he came to the U.S. on a student visa two years ago and has no priors. He's currently charged with one count of negligent child abuse.

(I)nadmissible or Deportable?

Because he was legally admitted to the U.S., the grounds of deportation apply.

(A)pplicable Grounds of Removal?

In reviewing the grounds of deportation, you identify "child abuse" and "crime involving moral turpitude" (CIMT) as grounds that this plea could trigger.

(C)ategorical Match?

You realize that this offense is not a CIMT since a CIMT requires a minimum of recklessness or intent and this statute only has a *mens rea* of negligence. However, you realize that this offense will be a categorical match for the deportation ground of "child abuse." You advise the client that if he accepts this plea, he will be deportable for a crime of child abuse.

This is a perfectly acceptable plea under *Padilla*. It analyzes the client's individual circumstances and provides the client a clear picture of the immigration consequences. Ideally, the defense attorney will go on to explore alternate pleas that do not trigger deportation, but if none are available, the client still has enough information to make a knowing, intelligent, and voluntary plea.

How Often Are Immigration Consequences "Truly Clear"? The 20-60-20 Rule

In the above example, we can be reasonably certain that the plea will trigger deportation, but there are other situations where the consequences are not so clear. How often can we expect to be certain about the immigration consequences of an offense?

In my experience, this question can be answered by the 20-60-20 Rule:

- **About 20% of cases will CLEARLY trigger removal**

  In the child abuse example (or in the case of Mr. Padilla himself), the conduct proscribed by the state statute appears to fall squarely within the plain language of the immigration ground of removal. In these cases, it's good to review state-specific resources to confirm this and then negotiate an alternate plea. However, the reality is that there will be cases where the charges are so serious and /or numerous that no safe plea is available.

  Say the client was entering on a visitor's visa and the Border Patrol found 200 lbs of cocaine in the trunk. Any drug plea will make him deportable and ineligible to reenter on a visa in the future, and the prosecutor is not going to let him plead to a non-drug offense. The bottom line is that there's probably *nothing* you can plead him to that's going to allow him to remain in the U.S. In this case, your job is to advise the client of the immigration consequences so he can decide whether or not to go to trial. Remember: *Padilla* only requires that you *advise* on immigration consequences, not that you ensure the client won't *suffer* from them.

- **About 20% of cases will NOT trigger removal**

  There are certain types of offenses that do not trigger inadmissibility or deportability, such as simple alcohol DUIs or traffic tickets. However, just because a conviction doesn't trigger a statutory ground of removal doesn't mean it can't have other consequences. When a client is pleading to a nonremovable offense, be aware of the following possibilities:

- ***Client has "Temporary Protected Status" (TPS):***

  In the vast majority of cases, removability will be controlled by the grounds of inadmissibility and deportability. However, if the client tells you she has something called Temporary Protected Status, or "TPS," the immigration consequences will depend on whether the client has two misdemeanors or one felony. ***DO NOT USE THE THREE STEP PROCESS IF CLIENT TELLS YOU SHE HAS TPS.***

- ***Client is undocumented and the offense brings him to ICE's attention:***

  If the client is undocumented and in criminal custody, the mere fact that he lacks legal status will often be enough to initiate an ICE investigation and subsequent removal. Say the client is pleading to a simple DUI for which he'll do 24 hours in jail. Advise him that while this plea will not trigger a ground of inadmissibility or removability, it will likely bring him to ICE's attention and he'll be removed for not having legal status.

- ***Client's offenses can be considered for discretionary purposes:***

  If the client is or will be applying for an immigration benefit in the future, such as a visa renewal, permanent residence, or naturalization, a plea that does not trigger removal could nevertheless cause a denial of this benefit on discretionary grounds. For instance, if the client is a permanent resident applying for naturalization and pleading to a simple DUI, you may want to advise him that this will not get him deported but it *can* be considered as part of his naturalization application.

➢ **About 60% of cases will have a RISK of triggering removability that you may be able to minimize.**

Sandwiched in the middle of these extremes, there are a large number of cases that *could* trigger removability depending on how you plead. In these cases, you may not be able to erase all the immigration consequences, but you can frequently leave client a "legal window" that allows her to avoid automatic deportability or inadmissibility. We'll discuss how to do this later on.

Don't Get Overwhelmed or Discouraged!

When first attempting this three step process, it's easy to become confused and overwhelmed. But remember that many of the cases you see will repeat themselves, and as soon as you've done one, you can often apply the same analysis to others. For instance, if you handle primarily DUIs or domestic violence cases, you'll learn how a certain plea will affect a client with a particular immigration status and be able to recycle much of your research and analysis in future cases.

We've discussed the general outline of the three step IAC formula; now let's figure out how to do it.

Summary of important points:

- The three step "IAC" formula requires you to determine:
  1) whether the client is inadmissible or deportable;
  2) the applicable grounds of removal; and
  3) whether the conviction is a categorical match to the grounds of removal
- Under the "20-60-20" rule, about 20% of cases will clearly cause removal, 20% will not, and 60% pose a risk of removal that you may be able to minimize.
- Don't get discouraged: many of the cases you see will repeat themselves, allowing you to use the same analysis and research for other clients.

<u>Chapter Five:</u>

STEP ONE: INADMISSIBLE OR DEPORTABLE?

In this chapter:

- Determining whether a client is inadmissible or deportable
- Constructing a timeline
- Unusual types of immigration status

The first step in determining the immigration consequences of a conviction is to figure out whether the client will potentially be "inadmissible" or "deportable" as a result of the offense. This determination depends entirely on the client's current immigration status and/or the manner in which she entered the U.S.

Why Do We Need to Know the Difference Between Inadmissibility and Deportability?

The single most common thing that happens when I get a call or an e-mail from a criminal defense attorney is this: the attorney launches into a detailed description of the offense, the charges, the plea offer, and the client's family in the U.S. but says nothing about whether the client is here legally or not. I usually wait patiently for a pause and then interject: "And what is the client's current immigration status?"

Nothing else matters until you know this. Nothing. It's the first step of every single analysis I do or have ever done, and if the defender doesn't know the client's immigration status, I won't give one word of advice until he finds out what it is.

Why is this so important? Because the client's status tells us which set of laws from the Immigration and Nationality Act applies. And the set of laws that applies will frequently change the outcome.

Let's say I have a client who entered illegally but has a U.S. citizen parent who submitted a petition for him to get a green card. The client is charged with simple possession of a firearm. Since there's no ground of inadmissibility for firearms offenses and since simple possession of a firearm is not a crime involving moral turpitude, I can advise the client that this plea will not disqualify him from using his parent's petition to gain permanent residence. He won't even need a waiver.

But say I have another client who was admitted to the U.S. as a lawful permanent resident four years ago and is offered the same plea. Since any offense relating to firearms is a ground of deportation, I will advise the client that this plea will make him deportable, and since he hasn't had his green card for long, he won't be eligible for a pardon. While this plea won't have a huge impact on the undocumented client, it will almost certainly lead to deportation for the permanent resident. Therefore, the advice I give in each of these cases is 100% dependent on the client's immigration status.

Key Legal Terms

First, let's go over some of the terms. You may have heard the terms "removable," "deportable," and "inadmissible" seemingly used interchangeably. What's the difference between them and why do we use them sometimes and not others?

> **Removal** is an umbrella term for both "deportable" and "inadmissible." It refers to the general process of removing someone from the country, whether she's here legally or not. "Removal proceedings" often refers to a series of administrative hearings before an immigration judge.

- **Deportable** refers to a person who has been legally admitted to the U.S. but has somehow violated the conditions of that admission, either through overstaying a visa, being convicted of a crime, or some other type of violation. *A person must be physically inside the U.S. to be deportable.*

- **Inadmissible** refers to a person who is seeking to be admitted to the U.S. but is ineligible for reasons such as a criminal conviction, a medical or psychological condition, certain types of conduct, or having entered the U.S. illegally.

  A person can be physically inside OR outside the U.S. and be inadmissible. For instance, a person who entered the U.S. illegally was never admitted, and even if he's been here twenty years, he'll still be inadmissible when he goes to apply for legal status. Sometimes a person who has legal status can also be inadmissible; for instance, if a client was admitted as a lawful permanent resident and then travels abroad, he could be inadmissible upon his return for a criminal conviction.

In other words, "deportable" and "inadmissible" are two subsets of the term "removable." You'll often hear people use the word "deport" to indicate any expulsion from the U.S., but in this context, we're going to use "deportable" as a specific legal term.

So Who's Inadmissible and Who's Deportable?

Here's a list of the most common categories of people who may be inadmissible or deportable:

INADMISSIBLE

- Undocumented who entered illegally
- Lawful Permanent Resident (LPR) at a border or airport
- "Work permit"
- Person "paroled" into U.S.

DEPORTABLE

- Visa/Border Crossing Card
- Lawful Permanent Resident (LPR) inside the U.S.
- I-94
- Passport stamp

Let's take a closer look at each of these categories to help you identify the clients who are in them. For each category, I've included one or more questions you can ask the client to confirm whether she falls within this group.

Inadmissible

➢ **Undocumented who entered illegally**

This is a person who crossed into the U.S. at some place other than an official border entry or an airport, perhaps through a desert or a river.

Questions to ask: "Did you enter with or without papers?"
"Did you cross a desert, a river, or the mountains to enter the U.S.?"

➢ **LPR at border or airport:**

This is a person who has lawful permanent residence (LPR), also known as a "green card," but is returning from a trip abroad. If an LPR is ineligible to enter the U.S. due to past or present criminal conduct, she will be called an "arriving alien" and charged as inadmissible. Even if an arriving alien is permitted to enter the U.S. and is not immediately taken into custody, she may still be charged as inadmissible in any subsequent removal proceedings.

Questions to ask: "Are you a permanent resident?"
"Did you recently return from a trip abroad?"

"Were you arrested at the border or airport?
"When you returned, did immigration ask you a lot of questions and/or give you some paperwork?"

- **"Work permit":**

One of the most common and confusing situations involves a person who entered illegally, does not have a clearly defined status, but claims to have a "work permit." This frequently happens when a relative submits a petition for the client and the client is permitted to work while waiting to become an LPR. It can also signal that the client has something called "Temporary Protected Status" or has applied for asylum. However, employment authorization is *not*, by itself, an admission, and a person who has a work permit with no other legal immigration status would be considered inadmissible.

Questions to ask: "Did you enter without papers?"
"Do you have a card that allows you to work?"
"Did anyone ever put papers in for you or one of your family members?"
"Did you ever apply for asylum?"
"Are you from El Salvador, Haiti, Honduras, Nicaragua, Somalia, or the Sudan?"

- **Person "paroled" into the U.S.:**

In special circumstances, a person may be allowed to enter the U.S. temporarily to deal with a serious illness (his own or that of a family member), face criminal prosecution, serve as a material witness, or for other reasons. A person who is "paroled" into the U.S. has not been officially admitted and will be charged as inadmissible if removal proceedings are initiated.

Questions to ask: "Why did they let you enter the U.S.?"
"Did they use the word 'parole'?"
"Did they give you any paperwork?"

Deportable

- **Lawful Permanent Resident (LPR) inside the U.S.:**

In most cases, an LPR who is arrested and charged with a removable crime inside the U.S. will be considered deportable. Therefore, the biggest challenge is simply determining whether the status that the client has is lawful permanent residence. LPR status is often known as a "mica," an I-551, a resident alien, or a "green card." A person remains an LPR even if she loses the card or it expires.

Questions to ask: "Do you have permanent residence/mica/I-551/a green card/card that says 'resident alien'?"
"Where were you arrested for the current offense? (e.g. inside the U.S. or at a border or airport)"

- **Visa/Border Crossing Card**

There are a myriad of visas for students, employees, entertainers, tourists, and others, which can range from a few days to years. In most cases, a person will apply for and be granted this visa from outside the U.S. and use it to enter the U.S. Even if the visa has expired and the client has no current lawful status, he will be considered deportable since the *manner in which he entered* controls.

Questions to ask: "Did you enter the U.S. on a visa?"
"What kind of visa?"
"When does/did the visa expire?"

- **I-94**

An I-94 is an Arrival-Departure Record that temporary immigrants are frequently given when they enter the U.S. It is not a legal status by itself, but it reflects that someone has entered legally, usually on a visa or as a refugee.

Questions to ask: "Do you have a small white card in your passport?"
"Was this card stamped by an immigration officer?"

- **Passport stamp**

The U.S. allows people from certain countries (such as Canada and most European nations) to enter for up to 90 days by merely having their passports stamped. Even if the person has stayed longer than 90 days, she will be considered deportable since the manner in which she entered controls.

Questions to ask: "What country are you from?"
"How long were you told that you could stay in the U.S.?

Constructing a Quick Timeline

In addition to determining whether your client is deportable or inadmissible, it's also important to know how long your client has been in that category since certain grounds of removability will only be triggered by an offense that occurs within a particular time frame (such as a "crime involving moral turpitude" committed within five years of admission). Also, even if a client is removable, she may be eligible to apply for a waiver to stay in the U.S. depending on how long she's been here.

Try to construct a quick timeline that gives you an overview of the client's immigration history. For instance, a client may tell you that he's an LPR. But by asking a few more questions, you can determine:

1992 or 1993: client entered the U.S. illegally
1997: client married a U.S. citizen
1998: client's spouse submitted a petition
2000: client became an LPR

Don't expect to get the exact dates every time; most clients haven't memorized the precise chronology of their immigration history. Usually, the most important date to know is when someone became an LPR. If you or the client has a copy of the "Resident Alien" card, this will be listed on the bottom right-hand corner of the card.

Unusual Types of Immigration Status

About 95% of the cases you see will fit into one of the inadmissible or deportable categories listed above. But as always, there may be some confusing exceptions. If your client doesn't immediately fit into one of the above categories, review the following groups to see if any might apply:

- **Temporary Protected Status (TPS):**

  If there are conditions in a country that prevent its citizens from returning, such as armed conflict or a natural disaster, Congress may permit citizens of these countries to remain in the U.S. for a temporary period of time. During this time, they may apply for work authorization and may not be removed from the U.S. The most recent countries that have been designated for TPS are El Salvador, Haiti, Honduras, Nicaragua, Somalia, and Sudan. *Note: A person may lose TPS status if she has two misdemeanors or one felony, regardless of whether she is inadmissible or deportable.* ***DO NOT USE THE THREE STEP IAC PROCESS IF THE CLIENT TELLS YOU SHE HAS TPS!***

- **Asylees and Refugees:**

  Currently there is some question as to whether a refugee who has not yet become an LPR should be considered inadmissible or deportable, so the best course is to assume that the grounds of inadmissibility will apply. Also, try to avoid pleading to a "violent or dangerous" offense, since this will make the process of obtaining permanent residence much more difficult for the asylee or refugee. A person who has been granted asylum can have that status terminated if convicted of an "aggravated felony."

What's the difference between an "Asylee" and a "Refugee"?

An asylee and a refugee have the same burden to show that they would be persecuted on account of their race, religion, nationality, political opinion, or membership in a particular social group. However, a refugee met this burden *outside* of the U.S. (usually through the United Nations High Commissioner for Refugees), while an asylee met this burden *inside* the U.S. (usually through an application process or before an immigration judge).

- **NACARA and ABC class membership:**

  If a person came from a certain country and/or applied for asylum before a certain date, she may be a member of a class or eligible to get legal status on that basis alone. This is most frequently applied to people from Guatemala, El Salvador, Nicaragua, Cuba, and countries from the former Soviet bloc. Seek an immigration lawyer's assistance on these cases.

- **Special Agricultural Workers (SAW):**

  As part of a 1986 immigration law, many seasonal agricultural workers applied for temporary residence and later became LPRs. However, a small number of these people did not become LPRs, and in most cases, their temporary residence has since expired. If a client tells you that he received "amnesty" in the late 1980's, follow up by confirming that he later became an LPR. If not, the client may be charged as undocumented and subject to the grounds of inadmissibility.

- **S, T, or U visa:**

  If a client has been helpful or was willing to be helpful in a criminal investigation or prosecution, or has provided critical information about a criminal enterprise, she may have applied for or been granted an S, T, or U visa (you might even have encountered some of these people on the witness stand during cross-examination). Seek an immigration lawyer's assistance on these cases.

- **Final order of removal:**

  Even if a person is ordered removed from the U.S., the government may be unable to carry out that removal order if there is no repatriation agreement with the client's country or the country refuses to accept the client. This happens most frequently with people from China, India, Vietnam, Laos, Cambodia, Iran, Cuba, Sudan, and Somalia. Ask the client whether he has ever seen an immigration judge and been ordered removed. If the answer is yes, the immigration consequences of a plea will be less important since the client already has an order of removal.

- **Unknown status:**

  There will always be clients who claim to have some type of status that doesn't fit into any of the above categories. If you are stumped by the information the client is giving you, your best bet is to assume the grounds of inadmissibility apply. If it's a high stakes case, consult an immigration attorney.

Conclusion

By now, you should be able to tell whether your client was legally admitted to the U.S. such that the deportation grounds apply, or whether your client has not been legally admitted such that the inadmissibility grounds apply. Next, we'll take a closer look at those grounds.

Summary of important points:

- Clients who are "inadmissible" include:
  1) those who entered illegally and do not have current lawful status
  2) lawful permanent residents apprehended at the border or an airport
  3) people "paroled" into the U.S.
  4) individuals who have a "work permit" but no other lawful status

- Clients who are "deportable" include:
  1) those who entered legally on a visa, border crossing card, or passport, regardless of whether that status has expired
  2) lawful permanent residents apprehended inside the U.S.

3) clients who have been issued an I-94

- There are other quirky types of immigration status that may not appear to fit into either of these two categories.

Chapter Six:

STEP TWO: APPLICABLE GROUNDS OF REMOVAL?

In this chapter:

- Grounds of inadmissibility
- The "petty offense exception"
- Grounds of deportability
- Aggravated felonies

In Step One we determined whether our client would be subject to the grounds of inadmissibility or deportability. Now let's find out what those grounds are.

Grounds of Inadmissibility

As you recall from the last chapter, the grounds of inadmissibility are those that will affect people who have not been legally admitted to the U.S. They will also affect pcople who have been legally admitted and are returning from a trip abroad.

Criminal Grounds of Inadmissibility (located at 8 U.S.C. § 1182(a)(2))

- Convicted of, *or formally admits having committed,* a crime involving moral turpitude (CIMT) (except for single offense with potential sentence of 365 days or less and actual sentence of 180 days or less)*
- Violation of any law relating to a controlled substance*
- Two or more convictions with aggregate sentence of 5 years
- Reason to believe drug trafficker or assisting drug trafficker*
- Reason to believe trafficker in persons or assisting trafficker in persons*
- Prostitution*
- False claim to U.S. citizenship*
- Encouraged/assisted another alien to enter U.S. illegally*

*Indicates a *conduct-based* ground that can be satisfied without a formal conviction

"Conduct-Based" Grounds

The first thing you probably noticed about the grounds of inadmissibility is that almost all can be "conduct-based." This means that a formal conviction is not required in order to be found inadmissible.

"Oh, great," you say. "So even if I get a good plea, ICE can still look at what my client actually *did*? How am I supposed to control that?"

Don't worry: if there's a conviction, the immigration judge or adjudicator is bound by the conduct to which the client pleaded (although if the plea is silent on a particular issue, police reports and other documents may be consulted in some situations). If there's no conviction, a CIMT or a drug offense can only trigger inadmissibility if the client makes some type of formal admission under oath or to an immigration official, which is rare.

The five other grounds of inadmissibility (reason to believe client is a trafficker in drugs or persons, prostitution, false claim to U.S. citizenship, encourage another alien to enter U.S.) are more likely to trigger a ground of inadmissibility without a formal conviction. For instance, the "reason to believe" standard is often defined as "probable cause," so a case that couldn't meet the "beyond a reasonable doubt" standard in criminal law might nevertheless be enough to trigger inadmissibility.

The primary reason to be aware of the "conduct-based" nature of these grounds is so you can alert clients to potential immigration consequences that may not stem from a formal conviction. Say you're defending an LPR client who was allegedly caught at the border with several pounds of marijuana. The state's case is weak and they decide not to prosecute. It's a good idea to inform your client that, even though there's no formal conviction, he might still be picked up by ICE and charged under a conduct-based ground of "reason to believe" that he's a drug trafficker.

We've talked about the conduct-based nature of certain grounds of inadmissibility; now let's look at the grounds themselves in a little more depth. For each ground, I'm going to give you a general definition followed by what it frequently does and does not include.

Crime Involving Moral Turpitude (CIMT)

(8 U.S.C. § 1182(a)(2)(A)(i)(I))

A CIMT is defined as "inherently base, vile, or depraved," "reprehensible," *malum in se*, or conduct that violates norms and shocks the public conscience.

A CIMT (for inadmissibility) DOES include:

- a minimum of intentional or reckless conduct (though strict liability sex offenses against minors or failure to register as sex offender may be CIMTs)
- offenses with an element of fraud
- DUI with actual knowledge that license was suspended
- theft with intent to permanently deprive
- most aggravated assaults (deadly weapon, great bodily injury, etc.)
- sex offense with element of assault, abuse, or lewdness

A CIMT (for inadmissibility) DOES NOT include:

- a *mens rea* of negligence
- simple DUI
- a single CIMT for which the maximum potential sentence is not more than one year and the actual sentence is six months or less
- a CIMT committed when the client was under 18 and at least 5 years before application for admission
- theft with intent to temporarily deprive
- simple assault/battery
- DV assault/battery committed with offensive touching

The "Petty Offense Exception"
(located at 8 U.S.C. § 1182(a)(2)(A)(ii)(II))

The petty offense exception is a critical tool in determining immigration consequences. It states that a single CIMT with a potential sentence of 365 days or less and an actual sentence of 180 days or less will not cause inadmissibility.

The best way to understand it is to look at the potential sentence of your state's misdemeanor statute. If the maximum sentence is one year, you can assume that a single misdemeanor with six months or less will not trigger inadmissibility. If the maximum sentence is six months, a single misdemeanor will *always* meet the petty offense exception. But there are some critical caveats:

- Remember that the exception applies as long as there's only one CIMT. If the client has two misdemeanor shoplifting convictions, both will make her inadmissible.
- Remember that the petty offense exception will *only* waive the CIMT ground of inadmissibility. For instance, if the client is pleading to a single misdemeanor drug paraphernalia, the petty offense exception will not prevent inadmissibility under the controlled substance ground.

Controlled Substance Violation

(8 U.S.C. § 1182(a)(2)(A)(i)(II))

A Controlled Substance Violation is "a violation of (or a conspiracy or attempt to violate) any law or regulation of a State, the United States, or a foreign country relating to a controlled substance (as defined in section 102 of the Controlled Substances Act (21 U.S.C. 802))." This ground of inadmissibility is particularly harsh because no waivers are available (other than for 30 grams or less of marijuana). This means that a client who is convicted of simple possession of meth or cocaine will probably never be able to become a lawful permanent resident.

A Controlled Substance Violation (for inadmissibility) DOES include:

- possession of 30 grams or less of marijuana (may be waiver available)
- possession of paraphernalia (may be waiver if ≤ 30 grams of marijuana)
- simple possession of any other drug
- sale, transport for sale, possession for sale, or any other drug trafficking ground (will also trigger aggravated felony ground)
- any other offense "relating to" a controlled substance, such as a look-alike substance or maintaining a place for drugs

A Controlled Substance Violation DOES NOT include:

- a drug that is not listed on the federal schedule of controlled substances
- in the Ninth Circuit, an expunged first-time simple possession or equivalent (subject to change, use with caution)

Two Convictions With Five-Year Aggregate Sentence

(8 U.S.C. § 1182(a)(2)(B))

This is a fairly self-explanatory ground that ICE rarely charges since most convictions that meet this definition will also be CIMTs or controlled substance offenses.

"Reason to Believe" Drug Trafficker

(8 U.S.C. § 1182(a)(2)(C))

This refers to a person whom the government has reason to believe is or has been a drug trafficker or aided a drug trafficker. It also includes a spouse or an adult son or daughter who in the past five years has obtained a benefit and knew or should have known that it came from the trafficking. It can be met by a conviction for a drug trafficking offense or by conduct that meets a "probable cause" standard.

"Reason to Believe" Human Trafficker

(8 U.S.C. § 1182(a)(2)(H))

This refers to a person who the government has reason to believe is or has been a human trafficker or aided a human trafficker. It also includes a spouse or an adult son or daughter who in the past five years has obtained a benefit and knew or should have known that it came from the trafficking. It can be met by a conviction for a smuggling-for-profit offense or by conduct that meets a "probable cause" standard.

False Claim to U.S. Citizenship

(8 U.S.C. § 1182(a)(6)(C)(ii))

The ground for a false claim to U.S. citizenship is met when a person falsely represents himself or herself to be a citizen of the U.S. for any purpose or benefit under immigration law or any other federal or state law. A conviction is not required in order to trigger this ground, although convictions for unlawful voting or false representation to law enforcement could provide a basis for it.

Prostitution

(8 U.S.C. § 1182(a)(2)(D))

The Prostitution ground is met when a person is coming to the U.S. to engage in prostitution or has engaged in prostitution within ten years of admission. A conviction is not required in order to trigger this ground; however, a person with multiple convictions for prostitution will likely be found inadmissible. In some circuits, the definition of prostitution is limited to actual intercourse, so when possible, plead clients to other types of sexual conduct.

Encouraged/Assisted Another to Enter U.S. Illegally

(8 U.S.C. § 1182(a)(6)(E))

Encouraging or assisting another alien to enter the U.S. illegally is frequently defined as an affirmative act of help, assistance, or encouragement, which can include paying a smuggler, providing a false document, or lying to law enforcement. It arguably does not include mere presence at the scene. A conviction is not required in order to trigger this ground. A narrow exception for a single offense involving an immediate family member may apply.

Grounds of Deportability

As you recall from the last chapter, the grounds of deportability apply to people who have been legally admitted to enter the U.S. This is true regardless of whether the visa or other document that allowed them to enter has since expired (though the expiration of a visa will itself be a ground of deportability).

Criminal Grounds of Deportability
(located at 8 U.S.C. § 1227(a)(2))

- CIMT committed w/in 5 years of date of admission for which a sentence of one year or longer may be imposed
- 2 CIMTs not arising out of single scheme
- Aggravated felony
- Conviction relating to controlled substance (except for single offense of simple possession of 30 grams or less of marijuana)
- Conviction relating to firearms
- Domestic violence; stalking; or child abuse, neglect or abandonment
- Violation of a protection order
- False claim to citizenship*
- Encouraged/assisted another to enter U.S. illegally within 5 years of entry*

*Indicates a *conduct-based* ground that can be satisfied without a formal conviction

One CIMT Within Five Years

(8 U.S.C. § 1227(a)(2)(A)(i))

A CIMT is defined as "inherently base, vile, or depraved," "reprehensible," *malum in se,* or conduct that violates norms and shocks the public conscience. Note that a single CIMT is deportable if it is *committed* within five years of a formal admission to the U.S., even if the actual *conviction* occurs more than five years after admission.

A CIMT (for deportability) DOES include:

- a single CIMT with a maximum sentence of one year or more committed within five years of admission

- a minimum of intentional or reckless conduct (though strict liability sex offenses against minors or failure to register as sex offender may be CIMTs)
- offenses with an element of fraud
- DUI with actual knowledge that license was suspended
- theft with intent to permanently deprive
- most aggravated assaults (deadly weapon, intent to cause great bodily injury)
- sex offense with element of assault, abuse, or lewdness

A CIMT (for deportability) DOES NOT include:

- a single CIMT with a maximum potential sentence of less than one year
- a single CIMT committed over five years after admission
- a *mens rea* of negligence
- simple DUIs
- theft with intent to temporarily deprive
- simple assault/battery
- DV assault/battery committed with offensive touching

Dates Can Be Critical

- If you're unsure when the client was admitted or it seems like a close call, make sure to confirm the exact date of the client's admission and the date the offense was *committed.* Don't rely on the date of conviction.
- In determining the date of admission, make sure to use the date the client was *formally accepted* into the U.S. and not the date the client physically *entered.* Some clients enter illegally and aren't admitted as LPRs until much later, in which case the date the client became an LPR controls.
- For LPRs, the return from a trip abroad does not generally constitute a new "admission" such that the clock will restart for purposes of a CIMT within five years (though it *will* restart the clock for purposes of the smuggling ground under 8 U.S.C. § 1227(a)(1)(E)).

Two CIMTs Not Arising Out of Single Scheme

(8 U.S.C. § 1227(a)(2)(A)(ii))

A client cannot be deported for two CIMTs if they arose out of a single scheme of misconduct. Crimes that are committed on the same day and are alleged in the same criminal charging document will generally be considered part of a single scheme.
In triggering this ground of deportability, the petty offense exception does not apply,

and the potential sentence for the CIMTs is irrelevant. For instance, if both CIMTs have a maximum sentence of six months, they will still be deportable.

Aggravated Felony

(8 U.S.C. § 1227(a)(2)(A)(iii))

An aggravated felony is the ground of deportation with the most serious immigration consequences. It will make the client ineligible for almost all forms of relief, strip the immigration judge of discretion, and trigger a lifetime bar to future immigration status. If the client is deported and illegally reenters, it may trigger much higher sentence enhancements.

Most Common Aggravated Felonies

(full list at 8 U.S.C. § 1101(a)(43))

- Murder, Rape, Sexual Abuse of a Minor, § 1101(a)(43)(A)
- Trafficking in a Controlled Substance, § 1101(a)(43)(B)
- Certain Firearms/Explosives Offenses, § 1101(a)(43)(C) and (E)
- Crime of Violence ≥ 1 year actual sentence, § 1101(a)(43)(F)
- Theft, Burglary, Receiving Stolen Property ≥ 1 year actual sentence, § 1101(a)(43)(G)
- Fraud, Money Laundering w/ loss of $10K, § 1101(a)(43)(M) and (D)
- Forgery, Counterfeiting ≥ 1 year actual sentence, § 1101(a)(43)(R)
- Obstruction of Justice ≥ 1 year actual sentence, § 1101(a)(43)(S)
- Running a Prostitution Business, § 1101(a)(43)(K)
- Alien Smuggling under 8 U.S.C. § 1324, § 1101(a)(43)(N)
- Failure to Appear (with 2 or 5 year sentence, § 1101(a)(43)(Q) and (T)
- Attempt or Conspiracy to commit any of above, § 1101(a)(43)(U)

Whether a particular offense is an aggravated felony is a complicated question that is beyond the scope of this book. However, there are many resources you can utilize that we'll discuss in the next chapter. At a minimum, you can do a quick electronic search in your federal circuit court using the particular aggravated felony cite above to see whether there is any clear case law in your jurisdiction.

The most important thing to remember in dealing with aggravated felonies is that, while some are based on an actual sentence of one year or more, others are not. For instance, if a client pleads to possession of cocaine for sale and receives a sentence of six months, this will be an aggravated felony since the drug trafficking aggravated felony ground is based purely on the elements of the criminal statute, rather than the length of the sentence. However, if a client pleads to aggravated assault and receives a sentence of six months, this will *not* be an aggravated felony since the "crime of violence" aggravated felony ground – while similarly based on the elements of the criminal statute – also requires a minimum one year sentence.

Controlled Substance

(8 U.S.C. § 1227(a)(2)(B)(i))

A Controlled Substance offense is defined as a conviction for "a violation of (or a conspiracy or attempt to violate) any law or regulation of a State, the United States, or a foreign country relating to a controlled substance (as defined in section 102 of the Controlled Substances Act (21 U.S.C. 802)), other than a single offense involving possession for one's own use of thirty grams or less of marijuana."

A Controlled Substance conviction (for deportability) DOES include:

- possession of paraphernalia
- simple possession of any drug (except for first time possession of thirty grams or less of marijuana)
- sale, transport for sale, possession for sale, or other drug trafficking offense (will also trigger aggravated felony ground)
- possession of a look-alike substance
- any other offense "relating to" a controlled substance

A Controlled Substance Conviction (for deportability) DOES NOT include:

- a conviction for a single offense of 30 grams or less of marijuana for one's own use (but see Chapter Eight, "Advising on Travel Consequences")
- an offense involving a drug not listed on the federal schedule of controlled substances
- an offense that does not name the drug anywhere in the record (if the state list of controlled substances is broader than federal list)
- in the Ninth Circuit, an expunged first-time simple possession or equivalent (subject to change, use with caution)

Firearms

(8 U.S.C. § 1227(a)(2)(C))

A Firearms offense is defined as the conviction of "any law of purchasing, selling, offering for sale, exchanging, using, owning, possessing, or carrying, or of attempting or conspiring to purchase, sell, offer for sale, exchange, use, own, possess, or carry, any weapon, part or accessory which is a firearm or destructive device." The definition is extremely broad, and you should assume that any statute that has "firearm" as an element will be deportable.

"Deadly Weapon"

Many statutes do not specifically mention firearms but instead refer to a "deadly weapon" or a "dangerous instrument." If the factual basis (or the charging document) establishes that the weapon in question was a gun, deportability will be triggered. If the factual basis establishes that it was a knife or other weapon, rather than a gun, deportability will not be triggered.

Domestic Violence

(8 U.S.C. § 1227(a)(2)(E)(i))

A Domestic Violence (DV) offense must meet the definition of a "crime of violence" under federal law, which requires the "use, attempted use, or threatened use of physical force" or a felony that has a substantial risk that physical force will be used. Any domestic relationship included within the state definition will qualify.

A Domestic Violence offense DOES include:

- an offense under state DV statute that has an element of intentional force
- a DV offense with a reckless *mens rea* (in some circuits)

A Domestic Violence DOES NOT include:

- a DV offense with a reckless *mens rea* (in some circuits)
- a negligent *mens rea*
- offense committed against property
- battery/assault committed with offensive touching
- false imprisonment committed by deceit

Stalking

(8 U.S.C. § 1227(a)(2)(E)(i))

Stalking is not well defined in immigration law. Assume that the ground could be triggered by any typical harassment or stalking statute.

Child Abuse

(8 U.S.C. § 1227(a)(2)(E)(i))

A Child Abuse offense is defined as any offense involving an intentional, knowing, reckless, or criminally negligent act or omission that is maltreatment of a person under eighteen or impairs the child's physical or mental well being. Child Abuse is an *extremely* broad ground of deportability, and you should assume that most statutes that have a child victim as an element will trigger it. If the client is convicted under a statute that does not have age as an element but the record shows a victim under eighteen, this could arguably be deportable as Child Abuse, though this is still better than an age-specific statute.

A Child Abuse offense DOES include:

- any statute with element of child abuse, neglect, endangerment, or abandonment
- ANY level of *mens rea*, including intentional, reckless, or negligent
- use or exploitation of a child as an object of sexual gratification (see also aggravated felony ground of sexual abuse of a minor)

A Child Abuse offense DOES NOT include:

- an age-neutral statute (e.g. simple assault) with no mention of age in the record or factual basis

Violation of Protection Order

(8 U.S.C. § 1227(a)(2)(E)(ii))

A person who is deportable for Violation of a Protection Order is defined as an individual enjoined under a domestic violence protection order who the court determines has engaged in conduct that violates the portion of the order involving protection against credible threats of violence, repeated harassment, or bodily injury. This determination can be made by either a criminal or a civil court.

Violation of a Protection Order DOES include:

- a criminal or civil finding that protection order was violated
- a violation of the portion of the statute that *protects* against violence (even if the client's actual conduct was not violent)

Violation of a Protection Order DOES NOT include:

- a plea to violating a portion of the order that does *not* protect from harassment, threats, or injury (such as failure to pay fines or attend classes)
- violation of the visitation or child support portion of order

False Claim to U.S. Citizenship

(8 U.S.C. § 1227(a)(3)(D))

The False Claim to U.S. Citizenship ground of deportability is met when a person falsely represents himself to be a U.S. citizen for any purpose or benefit under immigration law or any other federal or state law. A conviction is not required in order to trigger this ground, although convictions for unlawful voting or false representation to law enforcement could provide a basis for it.

Encouraged/Assisted Alien to Enter the U.S. Illegally

(8 U.S.C. § 1227(a)(1)(E))

Encouraging or Assisting Another Alien to Enter the U.S. Illegally is frequently defined as an affirmative act of help, assistance, or encouragement and can include paying a smuggler, providing a false document, or lying to law enforcement. It arguably does not include mere presence at the scene. A conviction is not required.

Avoid the most common error!

When determining the immigration consequences of a crime, a common mistake is to focus exclusively on CIMTs and aggravated felonies. Many defense attorneys assume, for instance, that since a drug or a child abuse offense is not a CIMT or an aggravated felony, it won't cause immigration problems.

In reality, offenses such as drugs, domestic violence, child abuse, or firearms constitute their own grounds of removability and can trigger the same immigration consequences as CIMTs or aggravated felonies. Say your client is offered a plea to simple possession of meth. You correctly conclude that simple drug possession is not a CIMT or an aggravated felony and advise the client that it will not have immigration consequences. However, this conviction – even though not a CIMT or an aggravated felony – will trigger the separate and distinct controlled substance ground of removability. ***In other words, drugs, DV, firearms, child abuse and all the other categories listed above are not subsets of CIMTs and aggravated felonies; they constitute their own independent grounds of removal.***

Grounds of removability at a glance:

Inadmissibility

- CIMT
- Controlled substance
- Two convictions w/ 5 years
- Reason to believe drug trafficker
- Reason to believe human trafficker
- Prostitution
- False claim to U.S. citizenship
- Encourage other to enter illegally

Deportability

- CIMT w/in 5 years
- 2 CIMTs
- Controlled substance
- Aggravated felony
- Firearms
- DV/stalking/child abuse
- Violation of protection order
- False claim to citizenship
- Encourage other to enter illegally

Aggravated Felonies

- Murder, Rape, Sexual Abuse of a Minor
- Drug Trafficking
- Certain Firearms/Explosives offenses
- Crime of Violence ≥ 1 year
- Theft, Burglary, Rec. Stolen Prop. ≥ 1 year
- Fraud w/ loss of $10K
- Forgery, Counterfeiting ≥ 1 year
- Obstruction of Justice ≥ 1 year
- Running Prostitution Business
- Alien Smuggling per 8 U.S.C. § 1324
- Failure to Appear
- Attempt/Conspiracy to commit above

You'll notice that some offenses are listed in both the grounds of inadmissibility and deportability (e.g., CIMT, controlled substance, false claim to citizenship, encouraging another to enter U.S.). Others appear only as a ground of inadmissibility (e.g., "reason to believe" trafficker or prostitution). Others appear only as a ground of deportability (e.g. aggravated felony, firearms, DV, child abuse, violation of a protection order). This is why Step One required us to determine whether the client is inadmissible or deportable, since we can't know the immigration consequences of an offense until we know which set of grounds will apply.

Our job in Step Three is to determine whether one or more of these grounds will *actually* be triggered by the plea. It's not always easy or conclusive, but I'll provide you with some tips and a variety of resources to consult. And if you've gotten this far, you can definitely make it the rest of the way.

Summary of important points:

- The grounds of inadmissibility include:
  1. a CIMT
  2. a controlled substance offense
  3. two or more convictions with an aggregate sentence of five years
  4. reason to believe drug trafficker
  5. reason to believe human trafficker
  6. prostitution
  7. false claim to U.S. citizenship
  8. encourage another to enter illegally
- The grounds of deportability include:
  1. one CIMT within five years of admission
  2. two CIMTs at any time
  3. a controlled substance offense
  4. an aggravated felony
  5. a firearms offense
  6. DV/stalking/child abuse
  7. a violation of protection order
  8. a false claim to U.S. citizenship
  9. encourage another to enter illegally

Chapter Seven:

STEP THREE: CATEGORICAL MATCH?

In this chapter:

- Definition of a "conviction" for immigration purposes
- The Categorical Approach
- Six ways to determine if statute is a "categorical match"
- The Modified Categorical Approach and Circumstance-Specific Approach

In Step Two we identified which grounds of inadmissibility or deportability might be triggered by the potential offense. The final step is to determine whether the plea will *actually* trigger these grounds.

Is Step Three Necessary?

Some people may question whether *Padilla* even requires a defense attorney to proceed to Step Three. Isn't it enough to identify the potential ground of removal and advise the client that she might bc deported on account of it?

As we discussed earlier, the text of *Padilla* would suggest the answer is no. While the decision acknowledged some situations in which the immigration consequences of a plea will be uncertain, it also noted that there will be circumstances where the consequences are "truly clear." Without doing Step Three, a defender will never know the difference. As such, a defender who merely counseled Mr. Padilla that he "might" be deported would be giving inaccurate advice.

A defender who doesn't undertake a Step Three analysis will also miss out on an opportunity to negotiate a favorable plea. Say your LPR client was caught with a pipe that had a small amount of marijuana in it and has been charged with possession of paraphernalia. A defender who only completed Step Two would merely advise the client that a plea to possession of paraphernalia would trigger the controlled substance ground of deportability. However, a defender who proceeded to Step Three might be able to negotiate a plea to simple possession of marijuana instead, which would not trigger deportation as long as the client didn't leave the U.S. A savvy immigration lawyer could certainly try to bring an IAC claim against the first defender, arguing that a reasonable criminal attorney would have done the minimal work necessary to plead to the equivalent offense that would not make the client deportable. In other words, failing to proceed to Step Three could in itself arguably constitute IAC.

Beyond IAC claims, however, it just makes sense to do the best you can on behalf of your client. I know this is challenging territory and your caseload is already overwhelming. But a few extra minutes of research could mean the difference between your client staying in the U.S. or being permanently separated from his family, job, friends, and the country he calls home.

Is it a "Conviction" for Immigration Purposes?

The first question we have to ask is whether the offense will even be considered a "conviction" for immigration purposes. It's critical to remember that immigration law has its own definition of "conviction" and is not controlled by the ultimate disposition under state law. Under 8 U.S.C. § 1101(a)(48), a "conviction" is:

- a formal judgment of guilt, OR
- where adjudication of guilt has been withheld, there has been:
    1. an admission or finding of guilt, *nolo contendere*, or an admission of sufficient facts to warrant a finding of guilt, AND
    2. the court has ordered some form of punishment, penalty, or restraint on liberty (including fines, court costs, classes, probation, jail, and community service)

Many states offer some type of deferred adjudication that, if successfully completed, will result in the charges being dismissed. However, if the above criteria are met, a state offense in which the charges are dismissed due to successful completion of a diversion program *can still be a conviction for immigration purposes.*

A general rule of thumb is that diversion programs that are resolved through the prosecutor will not be considered a "conviction," while diversion programs that are resolved through the judge will be (though there may be exceptions to this). If your diversion program is resolved through the judge, consider: 1) whether there is some finding or admission of guilt by or to the court; and 2) whether the judge has ordered the client to *do something.* If both are present, assume it's a conviction for immigration purposes.

What About Sentences?

If the length of sentence is relevant to determining whether a ground of removability has been triggered (for instance, an aggravated felony with a sentence of one year), here's a few important principles to keep in mind:

- In determining the length of a "sentence" for immigration purposes, time sentenced to probation does not count.
- However, if the client violates probation and is sentenced to incarceration, this will be considered part of the sentence. For instance, if the client has a theft conviction and is sentenced to one week of jail and three years of probation, this will not be an aggravated felony. But if the client violates probation and is sentenced to sixteen months in prison, this *will* be an aggravated felony.
- In almost all cases, the amount of time served is not relevant; it's the official sentence given by the judge that controls.
- A suspended sentence is still a sentence for immigration purposes. The exception is when the "imposition" of the sentence is suspended in lieu of jail time or some other punishment. For instance, if the judge sentences a client to three years but suspends the "imposition" of the sentence in favor of thirty days of jail time, the sentence is thirty days. But if the judge sentences a client to three years and suspends the "execution" of the sentence, the sentence is three years.

WHAT ABOUT JUVENILE OFFENSES?

Here are a few pointers for dealing with juveniles:

- Juveniles who are adjudicated delinquent have not been "convicted" of an offense for immigration purposes.
- A juvenile adjudication may trigger a conduct-based ground such as prostitution, violation of a protection order, false claim to citizenship, smuggling, or one of the "reason to believe" grounds. A juvenile adjudication may also be considered for discretionary purposes.
- A juvenile adjudication will likely not trigger inadmissibility for a coduct-based CIMT or controlled substance offense because the "admission" is of committing a juvenile delinquency, not a controlled substance or moral turpitude "crime."
- Juveniles convicted of an offense in adult court have been "convicted" for immigration purposes.

Is the State Offense a Categorical Match?

If your client's offense will qualify as a "conviction" for immigration purposes, the next step is to determine whether the elements of the state criminal statute are similar enough to the elements of the federal ground of inadmissibility or deportability that the offense will trigger removal. This is known as the "categorical approach," and it's often considered one of the most confusing, frustrating, and nerve-wracking areas of immigration law. Don't despair – it's not as hard to grasp if you understand the reasons behind it.

INCHOATE CRIMES
Inchoate offenses (attempt, conspiracy, etc.) will almost always have the same consequences as the underlying offense. Exceptions may exist for some solicitation offenses in the Ninth Circuit.

Here's the basic idea behind the categorical approach: federal immigration law uses a single definition of certain types of removable offenses (such as "theft" or "domestic violence") in order to promote consistency, and this is known as the "generic definition." However, state criminal codes frequently use a different definition of these offenses that may or may not match up perfectly with the federal "generic definition." If the state definition matches up perfectly with the generic definition, the ground removal is triggered; if it doesn't, we have to do more analysis.

For instance, a conviction for "burglary" with a sentence of one year is a deportable offense under federal immigration law. However, State X's burglary statute may encompass simple shoplifting while State Y's burglary statute doesn't. If federal immigration law were to rely on what State X and State Y each define as "burglary," then a person who shoplifts in State X would be deported for burglary while a person in State Y would not. The Supreme Court has found that Congress didn't envision such an inconsistent result. Therefore, we have to look at whether the *actual elements* of the state law match the *actual elements* of the generic definition used by immigration law to tell whether the client can be removed. We can't just rely on whether a state says it's burglary or not.

Let's try to conceive this visually. Here, the square represents the generic immigration definition of an offense while the circle represents the state's definition:

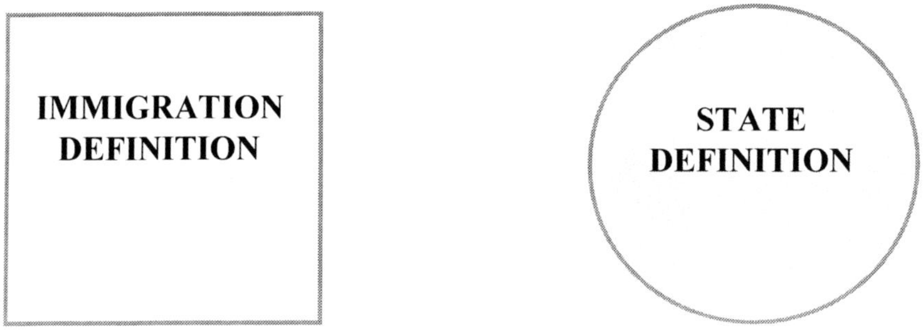

IMMIGRATION DEFINITION

STATE DEFINITION

If all the conduct reached by the state definition falls within the immigration definition, then a conviction under the state statute will categorically trigger the immigration ground of removal:

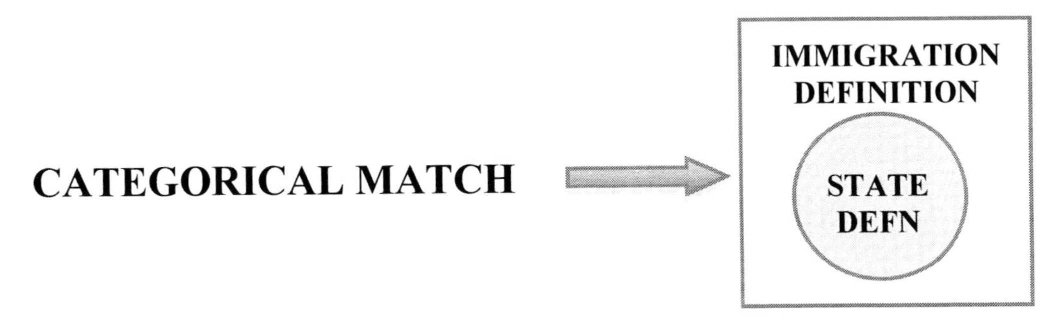

However, if there is conduct that the state statute covers that would not fall within the immigration definition, then a conviction under the state statute will NOT categorically trigger the immigration ground of removal.

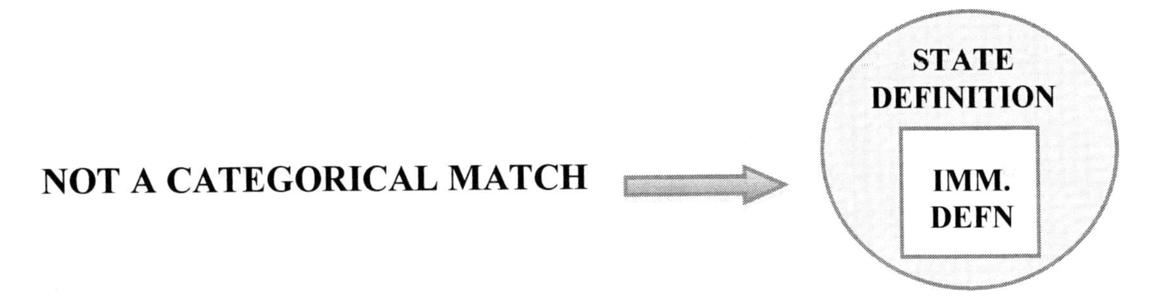

For example, the immigration definition of "burglary" requires an unlawful entry into a building or structure. However, California's definition of burglary includes a lawful entry and could also apply to non-structures such as a vehicle:

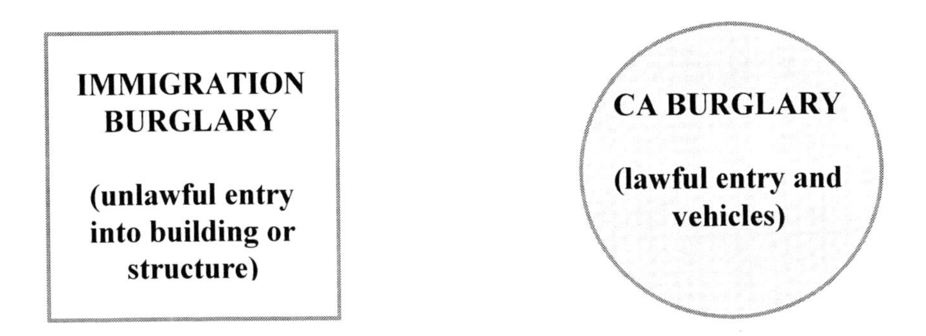

Therefore, California burglary is broader than, or is not "categorically," a burglary offense under immigration law.

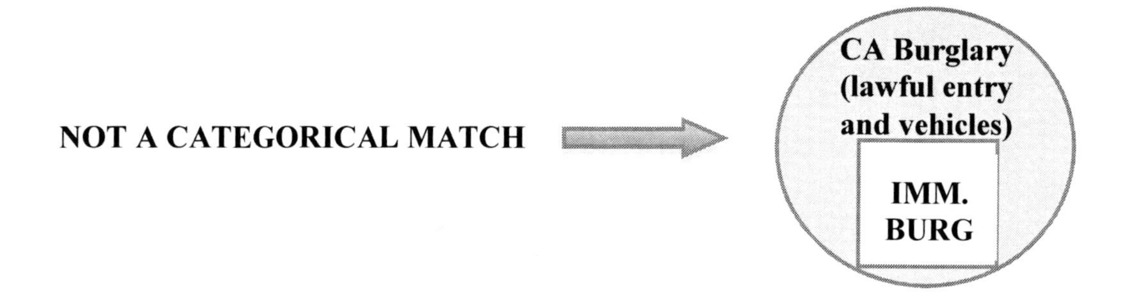

How Can I Tell if a Statute is a "Categorical Match"?

This is the most challenging part of the analysis. However, there are a variety of shortcuts and resources that you can draw upon to determine whether your state statute is a "categorical match" to the generic definition such that it will automatically trigger the ground of removal.

The best ways to determine a categorical match (from easiest to hardest) are:

1. **Consult state specific immigration chart**
2. **Compare the plain language of the immigration ground and state statute**
3. **Refer to descriptions of grounds in Step Two**
4. **Research immigration sourcebooks**
5. **Search Lexis or Westlaw for key terms**
6. **Search cases in annotated state code**

Here's a description of each method:

1. CONSULT STATE SPECIFIC IMMIGRATION CHART

Immigration practitioners in many states have created charts outlining whether the most common offenses from that jurisdiction will trigger grounds of removal. These charts can be very helpful in determining whether a certain state offense is likely to be an aggravated felony, a CIMT, a controlled substance or DV offense, etc.

STATES WITH REFERENCE CHARTS OF IMMIGRATION CONSEQUENCES
Available at http://defendingimmigrants.org/ (follow link to "Library")

- Arizona
- California
- Colorado
- Connecticut
- Federal
- Florida
- Illinois
- Indiana
- Maryland
- Massachusetts
- Nevada
- North Carolina
- New Jersey
- New Mexico
- New York
- Oregon
- Pennsylvania
- Texas
- Vermont
- Virginia
- Washington
- Wisconsin

These charts usually look something like this:

OFFENSE	AGG. FELONY	CRIME INVOLVING MORAL TURPITUDE	DOMESTIC VIOLENCE, DRUGS, FIREARMS, OTHER	ADVICE
§13-2904 Disorderly Conduct	No.	A6 might be charged as CIMT. Others not CIMT, but leave record vague as to facts	A6 is deportable fire-arms offense if record ID's firearm or explo-sive. Keep record vague. Also A6 deport-able as DV or child abuse against V where record shows domestic relationship.	Keep record open to possi-bility that A6 was not the plea, and keep details va-gue and free of egregious or violent acts, and it is a safer plea.

As you can see, charts may give you a good indication of whether a conviction under a certain state statute will trigger removal as an aggravated felony, a CIMT, or another ground such as firearms, controlled substance, or DV. It may also provide some advice on safer statutes or how to word the language of your plea to minimize immigration consequences. *Since immigration law changes quickly, make sure you're relying on the most recent version of your state's chart.*

2. COMPARE PLAIN LANGUAGE OF IMMIGRATION GROUND AND STATE STATUTE

The second way to determine whether there is a categorical match is to do a simple side-by-side comparison of the elements of the generic definition and the state statute. For instance, we know from Step Two that the generic definition of a firearms offense is:

> purchasing, selling, offering for sale, exchanging, using, owning, possessing, or carrying, or of attempting or conspiring to purchase, sell, offer for sale, exchange, use, own, possess, or carry, any weapon, part or accessory which is a firearm or destructive device (as defined in section 921(a) of title 18, United States Code).

Meanwhile, the state statute your client will be pleading to says:

> It is unlawful for an individual to carry a concealed handgun, knife, or other dangerous weapon.

On its face, the state statute is not a categorical match to an immigration definition of a "firearms" offense because it includes knives and possibly other weapons that are not firearms. Therefore, this statute is not a categorical match to the firearms ground.

DEFINITIONS ARE KEY

When looking at a criminal statute, don't forget to look up the definitions of the terms that appear in the statute. A statute that might seem to be a categorical match on its face may be broader than the generic definition due to the way a term is statutorily defined.

However, be aware that a statute may appear to be a categorical match when, in fact, state courts have interpreted it more broadly in practice. For instance, you might assume that a conviction for battery that has the elements of "force or violence" would be a categorical match to a "crime of violence" aggravated felony. But if a state court has interpreted "force or violence" to include offensive touching, such as spitting, this would not be a categorical match.

3. REFER TO CHAPTER SIX: APPLICABLE GROUNDS OF REMOVAL

In the last chapter, we went through a quick description of the grounds of removal and what may or may not trigger them. Say you have a client who's charged with a simple DUI and the only ground you think it might trigger is a "crime involving moral turpitude" (CIMT). You can refer back to the section on CIMTs in the chapter on Step Two, which states:

A CIMT DOES NOT include:

- a *mens rea* of negligence
- **simple DUI**
- a single CIMT for which the maximum potential sentence is not more than one year and the actual sentence is not more than six months
- a CIMT committed when the client was under 18 and at least five years before application for admission
- theft with intent to temporarily deprive

While these lists do not address EVERY issue that may apply to your state statute, they give a general overview of the ground of removal that may be enough to answer some basic questions.

4. RESEARCH IMMIGRATION SOURCEBOOKS/WEB SITES

There are a wide variety of resources in hard copy and electronic form that can help you determine whether your particular state statute will trigger a ground of removal. These are the ones that I have found most helpful and always keep at my fingertips:

- **Norton Tooby resources: www.criminalandimmigrationlaw.com**

  Norton Tooby is one of the leading experts on the immigration consequences of criminal convictions and has produced a library of books on crimes involving moral turpitude, aggravated felonies, post conviction relief, and other topics. His website listed above has free resources as well as a reasonably priced monthly or yearly subscription for access to the premium resources for research.

- ***Immigration Law and Crimes*, by National Immigration Project of the National Lawyers Guild, Dan Kesselbrenner, Lory D. Rosenberg**

  A comprehensive treatise on the immigration consequences of criminal convictions.

- ***Defending Immigrants in the Ninth Circuit: Impact of Crimes under California and Other State Laws*, 10th Edition with 2010 Case Update CD, by Katherine Brady, with Norton Tooby, Michael K. Mehr and Angie Junck**

A key resource for anyone practicing in the Ninth Circuit.

- **Defending Immigrants Partnership: www.defendingimmigrants.org**

  This joint initiative between the National Legal Aid and Defender Association (NLADA) and a variety of non-profit immigration organizations is dedicated to helping criminal defense attorneys represent noncitizens. The website has a library with helpful resources. Registration is free.

There are many other resources available, some of which may be particularly suited to your region. Ask a local immigration practitioner if there are books designed for your state or circuit that she has found to be particularly helpful. If you can't afford to buy some of premium resources, ask a local immigration practitioner if he'd be willing to donate a few books to your office when the new editions come out.

5. SEARCH LEXIS OR WESTLAW FOR KEY TERMS

If you have access to Lexis or Westlaw, do a search for your state statute (e.g. "ARS 13-1201") and the citation for the corresponding ground of removal below. Since different courts use either the citation to the Immigration and Nationality Act (INA) or its codification at 8 U.S.C., you may want to check them both separately.

For instance, say your client is pleading to providing alcohol to a minor under Anystate Revised Code section 18.2 and you want to know whether it would trigger a ground of removal as either a CIMT or a child abuse offense. Try doing a search for:

- "ARC 18.2" w/10 "crime involving moral turpitude"
- "ARC 18.2" w/10 "INA § 237(a)(2)(E)(i)"
- "ARC 18.2" w/10 "8 USC § 1227(a)(2)(E)(i)"

When researching, search primarily for decisions from the "Board of Immigration Appeals" (BIA), which is the immigration administrative appeals court, or from the federal circuit court in which you are located. If both have decisions on point, the circuit court's will generally trump the BIA's. State court decisions on whether an offense is a "crime involving moral turpitude" are not controlling for immigration purposes.

6. SEARCH CASES IN ANNOTATED STATE CODE

Sometimes the best way to determine whether your state statute will categorically trigger a ground of removal is to research whether anyone has been convicted under the statute for conduct that would not meet the definition of the immigration ground.

Say you're trying to figure out whether a conviction under your state's theft statute will automatically be a CIMT. We know from the Step Two CIMT description that theft with an intent to temporarily deprive is not a CIMT. However, your state statute just says "theft" with no mention of whether the intent must be to permanently or temporarily deprive.

If your state has an annotated code, skim it to see whether there are any cases in which a person was convicted under the statute for an intent to temporarily deprive (such as joyriding). If a single case exists, this will be enough to say that your statute is not categorically a CIMT.

> A state's annotated code may also list federal circuit court decisions determining whether that statute triggers a particular ground of removal

The State Statute Isn't a Categorical Match – Now What?

In any immigration situation, the best option is to plead to a statute that could not, under any circumstances, be a categorical match to a ground of removal. However, these statutes are often the less serious offenses that prosecutors won't accept.

Therefore, your next best option is to plead to a statute that is "divisible," or includes *some* conduct that could be removable and *some* that could not. If possible, specifically plead your client to a factual basis that does not match a ground of removal.

If you can't specifically plead to a factual basis that doesn't match a ground of removal, the next best thing is to plead to a divisible statute and leave the factual basis vague such that it will be difficult for an immigration judge or adjudicator to determine the conduct to which the client pleaded. Try to track the statutory language as closely as possible and do your best to avoid incorporating any outside documents (such as the police reports) into the factual basis.

Example

Say you're defending a client who is an LPR and is charged with carrying a concealed weapon. The statute includes "handguns, knives, or other deadly weapons." You want to make sure the client will not be deportable under the firearms ground.

BEST:	Plead the client to a statute that does not have firearms as an element, such as disorderly conduct.
2ND BEST:	Plead the client to carrying a concealed weapon, but affirmatively state in the factual basis that the weapon was a knife.
3RD BEST:	Plead the client to carrying a concealed weapon and state in the factual basis that the client was carrying a "handgun, knife, or other deadly weapon."

If you're able to negotiate a favorable plea, make sure the client has proof of it. Give the client a copy of any relevant document and tell him to show it to his immigration lawyer, the ICE lawyer, the immigration judge, and any adjudicator. If there's no way to give the client a written copy of the factual basis, tell the client to order a copy of the plea transcript and give him written instructions on how to do so.

What Documents Can the Immigration Judge Consider?

The types of documents that can be considered will depend on the approach used by the immigration judge.

- In some cases, the judge can only compare the *elements* of the generic immigration offense to the *elements* of the state statute. The conduct of the defendant is irrelevant, so any document apart from the statutory definition will also be irrelevant. This is called the **CATEGORICAL APPROACH.**

- In some cases, where the state statute covers conduct that both would and would not meet the elements of the generic definition, the judge can consider certain documents in the record of conviction, such as the complaint, the information, the indictment, the judgment, the plea agreement, the transcript of the plea colloquy, jury instructions, and any document establishing the factual basis to which the defendant assented. The judge will use these "record of conviction" documents to determine the offense for which the defendant was convicted and whether this offense matches the ground of removal. This is called the **MODIFIED CATEGORICAL APPROACH.**

- In some cases involving certain grounds of removal (usually "crimes involving moral turpitude" and fraud offenses involving a loss of more than $10,000 to the victim(s)), the immigration judge can consider almost any document in the record, including police reports and presentence investigations. This is called the **CIRCUMSTANCE-SPECIFIC APPROACH.**

How Do I Know Which Approach Will Be Used?

This is the million dollar question. The approach used will depend on: 1) the ground of removal; 2) the wording of the state statute at issue; 3) the jurisdiction where the client's case is being adjudicated; and 4) the immigration judge's analysis of the state statute. In other words, there are too many factors to know for sure which approach will be used, and thereby, which documents can be considered.

However, there are a few general rules you can follow:

Rule #1: When the potential ground of removal is a CIMT or a fraud offense involving more than $10K, assume that ANY document, including police reports and presentence investigations, can be used.

Rule #2: When the state statute contains various subsections or a list in the disjunctive, assume the formal "record of conviction" will be used.

Rule #3: When in doubt, try to keep damaging information out of the record of conviction and advise the client that the immigration judge *might* be able to look at anything in the record.

That's it. We're going to discuss several other relevant issues before we put all three steps together and figure out how to give the final advisal.

Summary of important points:

- **Definition of "Conviction"**

  Just because an offense is not a conviction under state criminal law doesn't mean it won't be a conviction under immigration law. If there has been: 1) a finding or admission of guilt by or to a court; AND 2) the judge has ordered the defendant to *do something* (such as classes, probation, fines), assume it's a conviction for immigration purposes.

- **Sentencing**

  Time sentenced to probation is not part of the official sentence unless probation is violated and the client receives an actual term of incarceration. Suspended sentences count, unless the "imposition" of the sentence was suspended in lieu of jail time or some other punishment.

- **Categorical and Modified Categorical Approach**

  Immigration law uses generic definitions of certain offenses, such as "burglary" or "crime involving moral turpitude." If the state statute includes conduct that both is and is not part of this generic definition, the statute is not a "categorical match" and is known as a "divisible" statute. When the statute is "divisible," immigration officials may be able to look to the formal record of conviction (charging document, judgment, plea agreement, transcript, and factual basis to which defendant assented) in order to determine the offense of which the defendant was convicted. In CIMT and fraud cases, they may also be able to look at police reports and presentence investigations.

- **How to Determine if State Statute is a Categorical Match**

  The best way to figure out whether a conviction under the state statute will be a categorical match to a ground of removal is to:

  1. Consult state specific immigration chart
  2. Compare the plain language of the immigration ground and state statute
  3. Refer to descriptions of grounds in Step Two
  4. Research immigration sourcebooks
  5. Search Lexis or Westlaw for key terms
  6. Search cases in annotated state code

- **What to Do if the Statute is Not a Categorical Match**

  If the statute is not a categorical match but you think there's a possibility it could still trigger a ground of removal:

  BEST OPTION: Plead to a statute that could *never* match the ground of removal.

  2ND BEST: Plead to a "divisible" statute and draft the factual basis for conduct that falls outside the ground of removal.

  3RD BEST: Plead to a divisible statute and leave the factual basis vague.

- **Predicting What Documents Can Be Used**

  If the potential ground of removal is for a CIMT or fraud involving more than $10K, assume that any document could be used. Otherwise, assume that the formal record of conviction (charging document, judgment, plea agreement, transcript, factual basis to which defendant assented) could be used.

Part III:

RELATED ADVISALS

Chapter Eight:
ADVISING ON TRAVEL CONSEQUENCES

Chapter Nine:
ADVISING ON RELIEF FROM REMOVAL

Chapter Ten:
ADVISING ON IMMIGRATION BONDS

Chapter Eight:

ADVISING ON TRAVEL CONSEQUENCES

In this chapter:

- Explanation of a "Travel Advisory"
- Determining travel consequences
- Client's transfer to another jurisdiction

Although we've finished the Three Step process, there are several other relevant issues that may affect your client's decision to accept the offered plea. These issues are: 1) where the client can safely travel if she takes the plea; 2) whether the client may still have a way to fight her case if she *is* removable; and 3) whether the client may be eligible for a bond while in immigration custody. This chapter focuses on the first issue of travel.

What Is a "Travel Advisory"?

A Travel Advisory is a warning to the client that the immigration consequences of a plea may change if the client travels outside a certain jurisdiction. As we've seen, there are distinct differences between the grounds of inadmissibility and deportability such that a conviction may trigger one but not the other. Therefore, a plea that is not deportable while the client is in the U.S. may still make the client inadmissible if she is at an airport returning from a trip abroad. Also, certain circuits have reached different conclusions as to whether an offense will trigger a ground of removability. Therefore, a plea that is not deportable in the Ninth Circuit may nevertheless be deportable if the client is in the Tenth Circuit.

WARNING:
Failing to give a travel advisory is the single easiest way to undo all the hard work you put into creating a safe plea!

Say you have an LPR client who was caught with a single marijuana joint and is pleading to simple possession of marijuana. Since the client has no drug priors, you correctly advise him that this will not be a deportable offense since it fits into the thirty grams or less exception in the controlled substance ground of *deportability*. However, if the client travels home to Canada next Christmas, he will be stopped at the airport and not allowed to reenter because the thirty grams or less exception does not exist in the controlled substance ground of *inadmissibility*.

Another example: let's say that your LPR client is busted for having cocaine in her pocket. In Arizona, you correctly conclude that a plea to Solicitation to possess cocaine is not a deportable offense since the Ninth Circuit has held that Arizona solicitation pleas cannot trigger the controlled substance ground of deportability. However, if the client goes to New Mexico on a business trip and has *any* encounter with law enforcement (even traffic tickets), she could be turned over to ICE and found deportable since the Tenth Circuit does not have a similar holding on solicitation.

Why Do I Have to Give a Travel Advisory?

The simplest reason for giving a Travel Advisory is that, without one, most clients will never suspect that leaving the U.S. or their particular circuit could have severe immigration consequences. Furthermore, most clients won't think about consulting an immigration attorney before a simple vacation, particularly if it's just to another state. You are probably the last attorney they will see before they travel, and if they don't hear it from you, they'll never be aware of the risks until it's too late.

At this point, it's unclear whether *Padilla* requires a Travel Advisory; the question will probably be whether a "reasonable" lawyer would have given one. To be safe, assume it's required. At a minimum, tell the client that travel can have risks and he should consult an immigration attorney before leaving the U.S. or the circuit where he resides. You can always download a map of the circuit courts and tell the client which states are in your circuit and which are not.

When Should I Give a Travel Advisory?

There are two common situations in which a Travel Advisory may be necessary:

1. The client has lawful status and is apprehended within the U.S. such that the grounds of deportability apply;

2. You encounter any circuit split in the course of researching the immigration consequences.

How Do I Give a Travel Advisory?

A Travel Advisory doesn't need to be a complicated process. Here's how to quickly do it for each of the above situations:

1. **Client has lawful status:**
   If the client has been legally admitted to the U.S., you probably determined in Step One that the client would be subject to the grounds of deportability. Go back and do the three step analysis again, this time assuming that the client would be subject to the grounds of inadmissibility. If a ground of deportability is not triggered but a ground of inadmissibility might be, tell the client not to leave the U.S.

2. **You encounter any circuit split:**
   While researching whether the plea will trigger a ground of removability, keep an eye out for anything suggesting that the consequences may be unique to a particular circuit. Most good reference books will contain tags on certain words of advice, saying, "if you're in the Ninth Circuit" or a cross-reference to a conflicting case in another circuit. If you're doing an electronic search, check your own circuit and then take an extra minute to expand the search to other circuits.

Giving a Travel Advisory doesn't mean you have to extensively research the law of every single circuit; it just means keeping your eyes open.

What If My Client is Taken Into ICE custody and Transferred to Another Circuit?

If your client is in criminal custody and has an immigration detainer (often called an "ICE hold"), she will likely be transferred to another facility after the criminal proceedings are finished. Since many of the larger ICE detention centers are in the south or southwest, it is not unusual for a client to have his immigration case decided in a different circuit than the one in which he was convicted.

How can you predict where the client will be sent? The simple answer is you can't. The best you can do is try to get a sense from local practitioners where the detained noncitizens from your area are usually sent. For instance, if you're in New York and you see many of your clients with ICE holds sent to Texas, assume that Second Circuit and/or Fifth Circuit law may apply and advise accordingly.

What If My Client Absolutely Has to Travel?

Some clients will vehemently object if you tell them they can't leave the U.S. or their particular circuit. Many of these clients have to travel as part of their jobs, while others merely don't like the idea that they can't visit family or friends. Obviously naturalization will cure these problems, so one option is to tell the client that he can travel as soon as he becomes a U.S. citizen. If the client is skeptical or still chafes under this advice, tell him to consult an immigration attorney to confirm whether travel will indeed be a problem.

Summary of important points:

- Failure to give a travel advisory is the single easiest way to undo all the hard work you put into creating a safe plea.
- To determine whether a client should receive a travel advisory, analyze whether the conviction will trigger a ground of inadmissibility. If it will, the client should not leave the U.S.
- Pay attention to any substantive law that appears to be unique to a specific circuit. If it is, advise the client not to leave that circuit.
- Try to determine whether clients from your area are regularly transferred to ICE custody in another circuit. If so, become familiar with any glaring distinctions between the law in your circuit and that circuit.
- When in doubt, tell the client to talk to an immigration lawyer before leaving the U.S. or your circuit.

Chapter Nine:
ADVISING ON RELIEF FROM REMOVAL

In this chapter:

- Does *Padilla* require advice on relief from removal?
- Descriptions of the most common types of relief, including the eligibility requirements and any criminal bars

Just because a noncitizen is taken into ICE custody and placed in removal proceedings doesn't mean she will be deported. Some people are eligible to apply for "relief" from removal, which means that they may be able to ask for a pardon or a waiver that would allow them to stay in the U.S., either temporarily or permanently.

Your first priority should always be to prevent the client from being deported *on account of the current criminal charge.* Many clients will already be deportable for a lack of lawful status or for prior convictions, but you want to avoid making their situations worse. However, if you can't keep the client from being deportable, your next priority is to preserve the client's eligibility to apply for a waiver or pardon that may allow the client to remain in the U.S.

EXAMPLE:
Joel is from Canada and has been an LPR for twenty years. He's arrested for having several baggies of cocaine and charged with Possession for Sale. The plea offer is to Attempted Possession for Sale of a small amount of cocaine. However, if Joel takes this plea, he'll be deportable for an aggravated felony and ineligible to apply for a pardon called Cancellation of Removal for Certain Permanent Residents.

It may not be possible for Joel to get a plea that won't make him deportable. However, if Joel pleads to simple possession of a large amount of cocaine, this will not be an aggravated felony. He'll still be deportable for a controlled substance offense, but since the statute contains no commercial element, he'll be eligible to apply for Cancellation of Removal.

Does Padilla *Require Me to Advise the Client on Relief?*

While *Padilla* focused on a defender's duty to advise on removability, it also cited past case law suggesting that counsel could "follo[w] the advice of numerous practice guides" to make clients aware of the availability of discretionary relief. But whether or not it's expressly required, advising a client about potential relief from removal is helpful because it gives the client information that's critical in deciding whether or not to accept the plea.

Say you have a client who is eligible to apply for LPR status through his U.S. citizen wife. He's offered a plea to an offense that will be a CIMT, and there are no good alternatives you can negotiate with the prosecutor. If you tell the client that the CIMT will make him inadmissible but that he may be eligible for a waiver, the client can decide to take his chances with the waiver, rather than going to trial. On the other hand, if the same client is pleading to a drug offense and he's informed that there are *no* waivers available for a drug conviction, he may decide to fight the charge more zealously. In other words, advising your client on potential relief will allow him to make a better-informed decision on the plea itself.

How Do I Know if My Client is Eligible for Relief?

Eligibility for relief sometimes depends on the client's current immigration status, as well as how long the client has been in the U.S., family ties, and various other factors. Here's a list of the different forms of relief:

Relief available if client is an LPR:

- Cancellation of Removal for Certain Permanent Residents
- Asylum-based protection (asylum, withholding of removal, or protection under the Convention Against Torture)
- Victim of domestic violence from U.S. citizen or LPR (VAWA)
- Claim to automatically acquired or derived U.S. citizenship
- Readjustment of status
- S visa (has critical information on criminal or terrorist enterprise)
- Voluntary departure

Relief available if client is undocumented or visa overstay:

- Cancellation of Removal for Certain Nonpermanent Residents
- Asylum-based protection (asylum, withholding or removal, or protection under the Convention Against Torture)
- Adjustment of Status

- Victim of domestic violence from U.S. citizen or LPR (VAWA)
- T or U visa (victim of trafficking or crime willing to assist in prosecution)
- Special visa for juveniles who've been abused, abandoned, or neglected
- Temporary Protected Status (TPS)
- Claim to automatically acquired U.S. citizenship
- NACARA (citizen of certain countries who applied for asylum before a particular date or is a particular class member)
- S visa (has critical information on criminal or terrorist enterprise)
- Voluntary departure

What Are the Requirements for Relief?

Each of these forms of relief has its own set of eligibility requirements that are summarized below, along with any *criminal* bars to eligibility. If the client wants to know whether she has a chance of staying in the U.S., scan the categories to see which ones might fit your client's situation. If you see any possibilities, pay special attention to the criminal bars in order to try to avoid them through the current plea.

1. CANCELLATION OF REMOVAL FOR LPRs

Overview: Allows an LPR who is removable to request a one-time "pardon." Judge will weigh the equities to decide whether relief is merited.

Who is eligible: LPRs who have seven years in U.S. after admission and five years with permanent residence. The seven years may stop accruing when removable crime is committed.

Criminal bars: Aggravated felony.

2. CANCELLATION OF REMOVAL FOR NON-LPRs

Overview: Commonly applied-for relief for undocumented persons, but very difficult to actually obtain due to level of hardship required.

Who is eligible: Undocumented noncitizens who have been in U.S. for ten years and whose removal would cause "exceptional and extremely unusual hardship" to U.S. citizen or LPR spouse, child, or parent. Must be extreme situation such as medical or psychological issue.

Criminal bars: Any conviction that would trigger a ground of removability (*may* be an exception for petty offense exception)

3. ASYLUM

Overview: Best type of relief to obtain for person who fears returning to her country of origin. Can lead to LPR status and allow family members to immigrate.

Who is eligible: People who have a history of past persecution or a well founded fear of persecution based on race, religion, nationality, political opinion, or membership in a particular social group. Must apply within one year of arriving in U.S. or within reasonable time after lawful status expires.

Criminal bars: Aggravated felony. Sometimes a drug trafficking conviction or a "violent or dangerous" offense even if it's not an aggravated felony.

4. WITHHOLDING OF REMOVAL

Overview: A form of protection similar to asylum that's more difficult to get and only provides that the person will not be sent to a particular country. No possibility of LPR status or bringing family to U.S.

Who is eligible: Same grounds as asylum but requires a "clear probability" of persecution, or a 51% chance. No one year bar.

Criminal bars: A "violent or dangerous" offense (which is broadly defined and could include DUIs), drug trafficking conviction, anything with five-year sentence

5. CONVENTION AGAINST TORTURE

Overview: Similar to Withholding of Removal but persecution need not be on one of five protected grounds.

Who is eligible: Person who is more likely than not to be tortured or killed by government (or possibly other group).

Criminal bars: None.

6. ADJUSTMENT OF STATUS

Overview: Process of acquiring LPR status inside the U.S., often through the petition of an immediate relative. Depending on status of petitioning relative and date petition was submitted, the waiting period can be anywhere from several months to 10-15 years. Even if deported, client may be able to continue process from home country.

Who is eligible: People who entered legally on a visa and have U.S. citizen spouse or child over 21, or who are under 21 and have U.S. citizen parent. Otherwise, eligibility will depend on date petition was filed, status of person who filed it, and manner of entry of client. Consult an immigration attorney before giving specific advice.

Criminal bars: Drug offense, CIMT, prostitution, false claim to U.S. citizenship, smuggling, aggregate sentence of five years, aggravated felony (if outside U.S.).

Waivers available: May be waiver for CIMT, prostitution or offense relating to thirty grams or less of marijuana if can show "extreme hardship" to family. A conviction for a "violent or dangerous" offense may require a higher showing of hardship. Apart from possession of a small amount of marijuana, *no waiver exists for drug offenses.* A single misdemeanor CIMT may not require a waiver.

7. VICTIM OF DOMESTIC VIOLENCE FROM U.S. CITIZEN OR LPR (VAWA)

Overview: Allows victims of domestic violence to petition for legal status without relying on abusive U.S. citizen or LPR spouses, parents or children to sponsor. Also known as VAWA (Violence Against Women Act).

Who is eligible: Person who has been battered or subjected to extreme cruelty by spouse, parent, or child who is U.S. citizen or LPR, or is the parent of child who has been battered or subjected to extreme cruelty by other parent who is U.S. citizen or LPR. Could also arguably apply to child who saw parent abused.

Criminal bars:	Must not be inadmissible or deportable.
Waivers available:	Possible waiver of conviction related to abuse. If not in removal proceedings, may be waiver for CIMT, possessing thirty grams or less of marijuana, or prostitution.

8. T OR U VISA

Overview:	Temporary visa with future LPR status for victims of trafficking or crime. Often used for DV victims if abuser is undocumented. Must have law enforcement, prosecutor, or judge who's willing to sign form.
Who is eligible:	Victim of trafficking or victim of crime who suffered substantial physical or mental abuse and has been, is, or is willing to be helpful in investigation or prosecution.
Criminal bars:	Yes, but broad waiver available for most crimes, will be discretionary.

9. SPECIAL VISA FOR JUVENILES WHO HAVE BEEN ABUSED, ABANDONED, OR NEGLECTED (SIJS)

Overview:	Provides LPR status to children who have been declared dependent on the state and are eligible for long-term foster care.
Who is eligible:	Children (usually must be under 18) who have been abused, abandoned, or neglected, and a finding has been made that it would not be in the child's best interest to return to home country.
Criminal bars:	Juvenile adjudication will not trigger bar. Conviction in adult court could trigger a bar, but waiver may be available.

10. TEMPORARY PROTECTED STATUS (TPS)

Overview:	A Congressionally-created temporary stay of removal for citizens of certain countries afflicted by civil conflict or natural disaster. Provides work authorization and temporary legal status; renewed every eighteen months.

Who is eligible:	Citizens of a particular country who were physically present in the U.S. on a designated date. Late registration may be available in some cases.
Criminal bars:	Ineligible for TPS (or will lose TPS) if convicted of one felony or two misdemeanors *regardless of whether they are CIMTs or would otherwise trigger removability.*
Waivers available:	No.

11. CLAIM TO AUTOMATICALLY ACQUIRED U.S. CITIZENSHIP

Overview:	If a parent or grandparent was a U.S. citizen at the time of a child's birth, the child may have automatically acquired U.S. citizenship without knowing it. Parent/grandparent must have lived in U.S. for certain number of years prior to child's birth.
Who is eligible:	Persons whose parents had U.S. citizenship at time of their birth, either through birth, naturalization, or automatic acquisition from *their* parents.
Criminal bars:	None.

12. CLAIM TO AUTOMATICALLY DERIVED U.S. CITIZENSHIP

Overview:	Client may have automatically derived citizenship if the client is an LPR and one or more parents was a U.S. citizen or naturalized before the client turned 18.
Who is eligible:	Requirements are slightly different for those born before 2/27/1983. Consult an expert before relying on claim to citizenship when accepting a plea.
Criminal bars:	None

13. ADJUSTMENT OF STATUS FOR ASYLEE/REFUGEE (209(c))

Overview:	Clients who entered the U.S. as refugees or were granted asylum after entering may be convicted of crimes that make them inadmissible to become an LPR. If so, they may apply for a waiver that would allow them to become permanent residents.

Who is eligible:	Refugees/asylees who can prove that a waiver should be granted for "humanitarian purposes, to assure family unity, or when it is otherwise in the public interest."
Criminal bars:	Can waive any conviction but may be unavailable if there is reason to believe the client is, or has assisted, a drug trafficker. If the crime was "violent or dangerous," a much higher standard of hardship may be required.

14. READJUSTMENT OF STATUS

Overview:	In some circuits, an LPR who is removable for a non-drug offense may be eligible to apply for a new green card in conjunction with a waiver for the ground of inadmissibility.
Who is eligible:	LPRs with a U.S. citizen spouse, U.S. citizen child 21 or older, or client under 21 with U.S. citizen parent. May also be able to use older petition filed by LPR relative.
Criminal bars:	Not available to waive drug crimes.

15. NACARA (Nicaraguan Adjustment and Central American Relief Act)

Overview:	A path to permanent residence for non-LPRs from certain countries who can show their removal would cause extreme hardship.
Who is eligible:	Citizens of Nicaragua, Guatemala, El Salvador, Cuba, and former Soviet bloc countries who entered the U.S. and applied for asylum or registered for ABC class benefits before a certain date. Very complicated form of relief – consult an immigration attorney.
Criminal bars:	Aggravated felony. Other crimes may require the client to demonstrate additional time and hardship.

16. S VISA

Overview:	A visa for those who possess critical, reliable information about a terrorist group or criminal enterprise. Commonly known as a "snitch visa."

Who is eligible:	Must have shared or be willing to share information with law enforcement. No application process; is completely up to government discretion.
Criminal bars:	None.

17. VOLUNTARY DEPARTURE

Overview:	Allows a noncitizen to leave without an official order of removal, which may make it easier to come back in the future if a legal route exists to do so.
Who's eligible:	Noncitizens not previously granted voluntary departure, given at the discretion of ICE or the immigration judge.
Criminal bars:	If requested at beginning of removal proceedings, aggravated felony is only bar. If requested at end of removal proceedings, must have been in U.S. for one year and have "good moral character" for last five years.

This list is not exhaustive; however, it encompasses the vast majority of relief that will be available to noncitizen defendants.

How Do I Advise My Client About Relief?

Determining eligibility for relief is a complicated process. The results will vary depending on the circuit law, the judge, the client's priors, the client's immigration history, and numerous other factors.

For these reasons, it's a good idea to be cautious in advising your client on eligibility for relief. Don't tell the client, "You'll be able to get Cancellation of Removal for this drug conviction." Instead tell the client, "It looks like you're going to be deportable for this drug conviction but you might be eligible to apply for a pardon that would allow you to stay in the U.S. There's no guarantees that the judge will give it to you, but I'm going to try to plead you to something that will ensure you're still eligible to apply for it." This alerts the client to a potential way he may have to fight his case without creating unrealistic expectations. It also lets the client know you're doing everything you can to help his immigration case.

Summary of important points:

- The most common forms of relief are:
  1. Cancellation of Removal for Permanent and Nonpermanent Residents
  2. Asylum, withholding of removal, Convention Against Torture
  3. Adjustment and Readjustment of Status
  4. Victim of domestic violence from U.S. citizen or LPR (VAWA)
  5. S, T, or U visa
  6. Special visa for juveniles who've been abused, abandoned, or neglected
  7. Temporary Protected Status (TPS)
  8. Claim to automatically acquired or derived U.S. citizenship
  9. NACARA
  10. Voluntary departure
- Do the best you can to maintain the client's eligibility for relief, but advise cautiously on whether she will actually be able to get it.

<u>Chapter Ten:</u>

ADVISING ON IMMIGRATION BONDS

In this chapter:

- Criminal bars to receiving an immigration bond
- Description of immigration bonds
- Should a client pay his criminal bond if he has an ICE hold?

If your client knows she'll be going into immigration custody, her first question may be whether she'll be eligible for a bond. Since there are very specific laws on immigration bonds, it's helpful to be aware of them.

Why Should I Advise My Client on Bond Eligibility?

The rules surrounding immigration custody are particularly harsh and can subject a client in removal proceedings to much longer periods of incarceration than the criminal conviction itself. For instance, it is not uncommon for a client to receive probation for a conviction for simple drug possession and then spend ten months in ICE detention fighting his immigration case without a bond.

What Crimes Will Make a Client Ineligible for an Immigration Bond?

The law governing eligibility for an immigration bond appears at 8 U.S.C. § 1226(c) and is controlled by the same analysis we did in Step One: whether the client is inadmissible or deportable.

AN *INADMISSIBLE* CLIENT WILL BE INELIGIBLE FOR BOND IF:

- Convicted of a CIMT (exception for single offense with maximum potential sentence of one year and actual sentence of six months or less)
- Convicted of a drug offense
- There is "reason to believe" client is a drug or human trafficker
- Client was apprehended at border or airport

A *DEPORTABLE* CLIENT WILL BE INELIGIBLE FOR BOND IF:

- Convicted of a single CIMT with an *actual* sentence of one year or more
- Convicted of two CIMTs
- Convicted of a drug offense
- Convicted of an aggravated felony
- Convicted of a firearms offense

If the client is **deportable**, a good rule of thumb is that any conviction that triggers removal will also make the client ineligible for bond *unless it's a single CIMT with an actual sentence of less than one year OR a DV/child abuse/violation of protection order/stalking offense.*

How Much Are Immigration Bonds?

The minimum immigration bond is $1500. In practice, the bond that ICE or an immigration judge sets will vary widely – in some areas, people consistently receive the minimum while in others the judges regularly set bonds of $10,000 or higher. For a client who has a legitimate way to fight his immigration case and is not subject to mandatory detention, a bond between $2,000 and $7,000 is common.

There are two ways to pay an immigration bond. First, the client can pay the entire amount of the bond, which will eventually be refunded as long as the client attends all her immigration hearings, complies with any final order of removal, and does not otherwise violate the conditions of the bond. Second, the client can work with a bail bondsman to pay a certain percentage of the bond amount (usually ten or twenty percent) that the client will *not* recover. In order to do the second way, however, the client or her family must own property that can be used as collateral.

What If My Client Can't Pay a Bond?

If the client flatly tells you that neither he nor his family have the money to pay a bond, preserving eligibility may not be the most important consideration. ICE frequently has the discretion to grant parole, so there's a small possibility that the client could still be released even without paying a bond. However, ICE's willingness to do this will likely depend on the severity of the client's criminal history.

Should My Client Pay a Criminal Bond if He Has an ICE Hold?

It depends. If the client is eligible for an immigration bond *and* has the money to pay both a criminal and an immigration bond, this may be a good option. However, if the client will be subject to mandatory immigration detention or doesn't have the money for both bonds, paying a criminal bond may result in the client being stuck in ICE custody with no way to resolve his criminal case.

Unless the client is definitely eligible for an immigration bond *and* has the money to pay both, it's probably not a good idea to bond out of criminal custody. While days spent in criminal custody can count as time served towards the criminal sentence, this won't be the case if the client is in ICE custody, and the client has little to gain by paying one bond only to be stuck in immigration detention.

If My Client Goes Into ICE Custody Before His Criminal Case is Resolved, How Can I Get Him Back?

The answer to this varies widely – some jurisdictions have certain procedures (such as issuing a bench warrant) that will convince ICE to transfer a person back to criminal custody. In other areas, ICE is reluctant to do so no matter what tactics you or the state court employ. Ask local practitioners what's worked for them but be prepared for the possibility that ICE may not be willing to bring your client back.

We've discussed how to determine the immigration consequences of a plea and how to advise on travel, relief, and bond. The last step is to put it all together in a conversation with your client.

Summary of important points:

- Most of the grounds of inadmissibility will also trigger ineligibility for bond, though there may be an exception for a single CIMT that had a maximum sentence of one year or less and an actual sentence of six months or less.
- Most of the grounds of deportability will also trigger ineligibility for bond, though there may be exceptions for a DV/stalking/child abuse/violation of protection order offense and a single CIMT within five years with an *actual* sentence of less than one year.

- Unless the client is definitely eligible for an immigration bond *and* has the money to pay both the criminal and immigration bonds, it's probably not a good idea to try to bond out of criminal custody.

Part IV

PUTTING IT ALL TOGETHER

Chapter Eleven:
GIVING THE ADVISAL

In this chapter:

- Three Rules for explaining immigration consequences to a client
- Two page Summary of the advisal
- Applying the three step formula to a hypothetical case

So now you've used the three step process to figure out the immigration consequences of the plea at hand. You also know whether the client can travel, if he's eligible for relief, and whether he can get an immigration bond. How do you convey this information to a client in a way that he'll understand? Especially when you can barely understand it yourself?

Explaining the immigration consequences of a plea is an art in itself. Here's three important rules to remember:

Three Rules for Explaining Immigration Consequences to Your Client

1. **Advise conservatively**
2. **Use the right language**
3. **Put it in writing**

What do these rules mean?

1. Advise Conservatively

If there is *any* potential for a different interpretation of the law that controls your client's immigration case, err on the side of caution. ICE officials and immigration judges frequently take a hard line approach and may disagree with even the most well established legal argument. So it's a good idea to *always* tell the client if there's a risk he could be picked up by ICE.

Say you have a long time LPR who's charged with domestic violence. You consult a chart and other materials and determine that if you plead the client to a factual basis with a *mens rea* of recklessness, it shouldn't make him deportable. Don't tell the client, "This plea won't make you deportable." Tell the client, "There's a good chance ICE will pick you up and try to say that you're deportable. However, I'm going to put some specific language in the plea so that if this happens, you'll have strong arguments you're not deportable."

Explaining the plea in this way has several advantages. First, you've psychologically prepared the client for the possibility that ICE may take him into custody, and the client is less likely to feel shock and anger if this does happen. Second, you've conveyed to the client that you're fighting for him, that you've gone out of your way to do the best you can for his immigration case.

2. Use the Right Language

Defenders frequently tell their clients, "This plea won't have immigration consequences." Try to avoid this phrase. It's inaccurate, since even the most minor infraction can be taken into account when applying for benefits such as a visa, a green card, or naturalization. For instance, if your LPR client is pleading to a simple DUI, you might be tempted to say, "This won't have immigration consequences." However, if the client's application for naturalization is denied because of the DUI, the client may believe you misadvised him since it *did* have an immigration consequence, even though it wasn't deportation.

A better way to phrase advice is to put it in the context of whether the client will be *deportable as a result of the conviction,* or whether the client will be *ineligible to get legal status as a result of the conviction.* For instance, you could tell the LPR client, "This DUI won't make you deportable, but immigration officials can consider it if you apply for naturalization." In cases where a conviction could have discretionary consequences, encourage the client to carefully comply with all fines, classes, and probation requirements since this can mitigate some of the negative effects.

As ramped-up enforcement efforts bring ICE into more jails and state courts, it's also important to remind undocumented clients that even if an offense is not removable, the encounter with law enforcement may be enough to trigger removal due to the person's lack of lawful status. It may seem obvious but many people don't understand that, even if they get a "safe" plea, this doesn't prevent ICE from investigating whether they are removable for other reasons. This also applies to legal immigrants who are removable for old convictions but have managed to fly under the radar for many years. As a best practice, it's always good to warn a client if you see a reason he could be removed, even if it's unrelated to your current case, since this can psychologically prepare the client for ICE apprehension and make it less likely that he'll blame you.

3. Put It In Writing

Under *Padilla,* it's going to be necessary to keep good records of the advice you provide to clients. The best practice is to fill out an intake sheet with all the immigration info the client has given you, your analysis, and what you told the client. Make a copy, give it to the client, have the client sign an acknowledgment that he received it, and then keep the original on file.

If you have specifically negotiated a plea to try to avoid immigration consequences, it's *extremely* helpful to give the client a separate written explanation of this, along with any relevant documents. Say the client is charged with domestic violence against his spouse but you're able to plead to a simple assault against a neighbor who was at the scene in order to avoid removability on DV grounds. Give the client something in writing that simply says, "Although Mr. X was charged with DV, he accepted a plea to simple assault against Mr. Y, a neighbor," then sign it as his defense attorney. Tell the client to wave this paper in the face of any immigration attorney, ICE official, or immigration judge that he encounters. At the very least, this will alert the right people that there may be a legal issue to investigate so that your hard work doesn't go to waste.

Keeping these suggestions in mind, let's review the entire three step process and corollary advisals, then apply them to a hypothetical case:

TWO-PAGE SUMMARY OF "THE ADVISAL"

Step 1: Inadmissible or Deportable? (p. 27-35)

INADMISSIBLE (p. 29-30)

- Undocumented (p. 29)
- Lawful Permanent Resident (LPR) at border or airport (p. 29)
- "Work permit" (p. 30)
- Person "paroled" into U.S. (p. 30)

DEPORTABLE (p. 30-31)

- Visa/Border Crossing Card (p. 31)
- Lawful Permanent Resident (LPR) inside the U.S. (p. 30)
- I-94 (p. 31)
- Passport stamp (p. 31)

Step 2: Applicable Grounds of Removal (p. 37-50)

Criminal Grounds of Inadmissibility (p. 37-41)

- Convicted of, or formally admits having committed, a crime involving moral turpitude (CIMT) (except for petty offense exception) (p. 38)
- Violation of any law relating to a controlled substance (p. 40)
- Reason to believe drug trafficker or assisting drug trafficker (p. 41)
- Reason to believe trafficker in persons or assisting trafficker in persons (p. 41)
- Prostitution (p. 41)
- False claim to U.S. citizenship (p. 41)
- Encouraged/assisted another alien to enter U.S. illegally (p. 41)

Criminal Grounds of Deportability (p. 42-48)

- CIMT w/in 5 years of admission w/ 1-year potential sentence (p. 42)
- 2 CIMTs at any time (p. 43)
- Aggravated felony (p. 44)
- Controlled substance (exception for 30 grams of MJ) (p. 45)
- Conviction relating to firearms (p. 46)
- Crime of domestic violence, stalking, or child abuse (p. 46-47)
- Violation of a protection order (p. 47)
- False claim to citizenship (p. 48)
- Encouraged/assisted another alien to enter U.S. illegally (p. 48)

Most Common Aggravated Felonies (p. 44)

- Murder, Rape, Sexual Abuse of a Minor
- Trafficking in a Controlled Substance
- Certain Firearms/Explosives Offenses
- Crime of Violence ≥ 1 year actual sentence
- Theft/Burglary/Receiving Stolen Property ≥ 1 year actual sentence
- Fraud/Money Laundering w/ loss of $10K to victim
- Forgery/Counterfeiting ≥ 1 year actual sentence
- Obstruction of Justice ≥ 1 year actual sentence
- Running a Prostitution Business
- Alien Smuggling under 8 U.S.C. § 1324
- Failure to Appear (with 2 or 5 year sentence)
- Attempt or Conspiracy to commit any of above

Step 3: Categorical Match? (p. 51-64)

1. Consult state-specific immigration chart (p. 56)
2. Compare plain language of immigration ground and state statute (p. 58)
3. Refer to descriptions of grounds in Step Two (p. 58)
4. Research immigration sourcebooks (p. 59)
5. Search Lexis or Westlaw for key terms (p. 60)
6. Search cases in annotated state code (p. 60)

Advise on Travel Outside U.S. and Circuit (p. 67-70)

Advise on Relief from Removal (p. 71-80)

- Cancellation of Removal for Permanent and Nonpermanent Residents (p. 73)
- Asylum, Withholding of Removal, Convention Against Torture (p. 74)
- Adjustment and Readjustment of Status (p. 75, 77, 78)
- Victim of domestic violence from U.S. citizen or LPR (p. 75)
- S, T, or U visa (p. 76, 78)
- Special visa for juveniles who've been abused, abandoned, or neglected (p. 76)
- Temporary Protected Status (TPS) (p. 76)
- Claim to automatically acquired or derived U.S. citizenship (p. 77)
- NACARA (p. 78)
- Voluntary departure (p. 79)

Advise on Immigration Bond (p. 81-84)

Hypothetical:

Using the summary on the previous two pages, let's analyze a case from start to finish using the three step analysis:

Laura works as a cashier at a clothing store and has been accused of stealing $1,500 of merchandise since she started in January 2010. She's charged with theft and offered a plea to the following statute:

> A person commits theft if the person knowingly takes the property of another, either temporarily or permanently, without consent or by means of material misrepresentation, with intent to deprive the other person of such property.

The statute carries a maximum of 1.5 years but the prosecutor has offered a stipulation to probation.

All we know is that Laura is not a U.S. citizen. How do we advise her on the immigration consequences of this plea?

Getting Information:

At a minimum, we need to know the answers to the Five Absolutely Critical Questions (see pg. 9):

1. When did Laura last enter the U.S.?
2. How did she enter? (e.g. illegally, visa, "green card," parole)
3. Did she ever get a green card, visa, or other legal permission to be here? If so, when did she get it?
4. Has she ever been deported or put into removal proceedings?
5. What priors does she have? (including misdemeanors)

Laura tells us that she first came to the U.S. on a visa in 2000 and received her green card in 2002. The last time she left the U.S. was for two weeks in 2008 to visit family and she reentered legally. She's never been deported or put into removal proceedings. She has one prior for driving without insurance from 2005. So our timeline for Laura will look like this:

> 2000: entered on visa
> 2002: became LPR
> 2005: driving without insurance
> 2008: left U.S. briefly
> 2010: committed theft

Three Step Analysis of Immigration Consequences:

Step 1: Inadmissible or Deportable?

Laura entered on a visa and is currently an LPR who was apprehended *inside* the U.S. Therefore, the grounds of deportability will apply.

INADMISSIBLE

- Undocumented who entered illegally
- Lawful Permanent Resident (LPR) at border or airport
- "Work permit"
- Person "paroled" into U.S.

DEPORTABLE

- Visa/Border Crossing Card
- ***Lawful Permanent Resident (LPR) inside the U.S.***
- I-94
- Passport stamp

Step 2: Applicable Grounds of Removal

If Laura pleads guilty to theft, we need to consider whether it could potentially trigger: 1) a CIMT within five years; 2) two CIMTs (with the prior); 3) an aggravated felony theft offense; and/or 4) an aggravated felony fraud offense.

Criminal Grounds of Deportability

- ***CIMT committed w/in five years of date of admission for which a sentence of one year or longer may be imposed***
- ***2 CIMTs at any time***
- ***Aggravated felony***
- Conviction relating to controlled substance (except for single offense of simple possession of 30 grams or less of marijuana)
- Conviction relating to firearms
- Crime of domestic violence; stalking; or child abuse, neglect or abandonment
- Violation of a protection order
- False claim to citizenship
- Encouraged/assisted another alien to enter U.S. illegally

Most Common Aggravated Felonies
(full list at 8 U.S.C. § 1101(a)(43)

- Murder, Rape, Sexual Abuse of a Minor
- Trafficking in a Controlled Substance
- Certain Firearms/Explosives offenses
- Crime of Violence ≥ 1 year actual sentence
- ***Theft/Burglary/Receiving Stolen Property ≥ 1 year actual sentence***
- ***Fraud/Money Laundering w/ loss of $10K to victim***
- Forgery/Counterfeiting ≥ 1 year actual sentence
- Obstruction of Justice ≥ 1 year actual sentence
- Running a Prostitution Business
- Alien Smuggling under 8 U.S.C. § 1324
- Failure to Appear (with 2 or 5 year sentence)
- Attempt or Conspiracy to commit any of above

Step 3: Categorical Match?

To be completely safe, we'll analyze every potential ground to see if it would actually trigger the ground of deportability:

- ***CIMT committed within five years of date of admission for which a sentence of one year or longer may be imposed***

  We know that a sentence of one year or longer may be imposed since the potential sentence is 1.5 years. However, we're not sure whether a conviction under the theft statute would be a CIMT since it may depend on whether there was an intent to permanently, versus temporarily, deprive the store of its merchandise (see p. 42-43).

  But even assuming it *is* a CIMT, the offense was not committed within five years of the date of admission. Laura's date of admission is her entry on a visa in 2000 (neither her transition to LPR status in 2002 nor her reentry in 2008 after a brief trip abroad counts as a new "admission"). Since the offense was "committed" in 2010 when she started working at the store, there were at least ten years between her last admission and the date of commission. Therefore, this plea won't make her deportable for a CIMT within five years of admission.

- ***Two CIMTs at any time***

  Driving without a license is usually a regulatory traffic offense that should not be a CIMT (see p. 42-43). But if you have any doubts, it would be a good idea to plead Laura to either a temporary deprivation on the current theft charge or at least leave it vague by pleading to a "temporary or permanent deprivation." Pleading Laura to a temporary deprivation would also be helpful in case she is ever convicted of a CIMT in the future.

- ***Aggravated felony***

  Laura could potentially be charged with either a theft or a fraud aggravated felony. However, since we're stipulating to probation, it's very unlikely that she would receive an *actual* sentence of one year or more such that the offense would be a theft aggravated felony. Since the amount of loss was no greater than $1,500, the plea could not be a fraud aggravated felony

After analyzing all the applicable grounds, it doesn't appear that any of them will be triggered. Therefore, this should be a "safe" plea for Laura.

Travel, Bond, and Relief?

Would it change the analysis if Laura were to travel outside the U.S. and apply for reentry at a border or an airport?

The answer is yes. While Laura needs two CIMTs to be deported from inside the U.S., she can be found inadmissible for only one CIMT if she's returning from a trip abroad. This plea will not fit the petty offense exception since it has a potential sentence of 1.5 years. Therefore, ***it is extremely important that we tell Laura not to leave the U.S.*** Laura may still be able to naturalize at some point in the future, at which point she could safely leave the country.

As long as Laura doesn't leave the U.S. and doesn't violate probation, she shouldn't be deportable. Therefore, we don't really need to advise on her eligibility for immigration bond or relief from removal.

How Do We Explain All This to Laura?

Incorporating the tips from the beginning of this chapter, here's one way to explain the immigration consequences of this plea to Laura:

> "I've looked at the potential immigration consequences of this plea, and if you decide to accept it, it's my opinion you will not be deportable. However, this is only true if you abide by some very important conditions."
>
> "First, this plea will *not* be safe if you leave the U.S., since the law is different for people with green cards who are returning from a trip abroad. Therefore, if you accept this plea, you *should not* leave the U.S."
>
> "Second, this plea will only be safe if you receive a sentence of less than one year. While I'm fairly sure you'll get probation from the judge, if you ever violate that probation and receive a sentence of one year or more, you will probably have an aggravated felony and there will be serious immigration consequences."
>
> "Finally, while this plea will not make you deportable, immigration officials can take it into account if you ever decide to naturalize."
>
> "There's always a very small chance that immigration will pick you up and say that you're deportable. I don't see any legal basis that would allow them to do that. But just in case they do, I'm also going to use some specific language in your plea that would give you strong arguments that this is not a 'crime involving moral turpitude.' If immigration tries to say it is, make sure your lawyer or the immigration judge looks very closely at these papers."

Fill out a form or type up a short letter with this information, including any efforts you made to plead Laura to a temporary deprivation in case it is ever charged as a CIMT. Have Laura sign an acknowledgment that she received this information and give her a copy of all the relevant documents. Congratulations, you've just provided your first effective *Padilla* advisal!

How Long Will This Take?

The first several times you give an advisal, it may feel complicated and time consuming. But over time you'll start to see the same types of cases repeating themselves and the analysis will become quicker and easier. And as you're learning the process, it never hurts to find an immigration lawyer who can confirm your analysis or provide guidance on more complicated cases. I've been working with some of the same defenders for years, and many of them can now figure out the immigration consequences of most pleas on their own and consult me on only very complicated or high-stakes cases.

It may feel overwhelming, but I promise: it can be done.

Summary of important points:

- Advise clients conservatively on immigration consequences. If there's *any* chance that ICE could say the conviction triggers a ground of removability, advise the client that she could be taken into ICE custody.
- Don't say that a plea will not have immigration consequences. Say that a plea will not make the client deportable or will not disqualify the client from obtaining legal status in the future.
- Keep a written record of what you've told the client. If you've done anything to try to avoid immigration consequences, give the client a written explanation of it.
- To provide an advisal that will satisfy *Padilla,* determine the immigration consequences using the three step "IAC" process. If relevant, give the client any additional information about travel consequences, relief from removal, and immigration bond.

Chapter Twelve:

THREE STEP ANALYSIS FOR COMMON CASES

In this chapter:

- Undocumented client with potential drug conviction
- Temporary visa with a DUI charge
- Undocumented client with false document charge
- LPR with potential aggravated felony
- Temporary visa with possession of marijuana charge
- LPR with potential CIMT within five years of admission

This chapter is designed to show you how to identify and analyze some of the most common scenarios under the three step framework.

Undocumented Client with Potential Drug Conviction

Marco is undocumented and entered the U.S. twelve years ago; he has never been deported. His wife is also undocumented and they have two U.S. citizen children. He's arrested for possession of cocaine and offered a plea to simple possession of a controlled substance. What will be the immigration consequences if he accepts this plea?

1. **Inadmissible or Deportable?**

   Despite being in the U.S. for twelve years, Marco was never formally admitted and will therefore be considered inadmissible.

2. **Applicable Grounds of Removability?**

   Possibly the CIMT ground, the controlled substance ground, and the "reason to believe drug trafficker" ground.

3. **Categorical Match?**

   - **CIMT:** Simple drug possession is generally not a CIMT.
   - **Controlled substance:** Simple drug possession will nearly always be an offense "relating to a controlled substance." The exception is if the state list of illegal drugs is broader than the federal list and

the record of conviction does not name the drug of conviction. (In the Ninth Circuit, a conviction under a specific Solicitation statute is also not a controlled substance offense.)

- **"Reason to believe drug trafficker":** Doesn't require a conviction so any proof could be used in immigration court. But unless there's evidence of Marco's involvement in the larger drug trade, simple possession will probably not trigger this ground.

Therefore, the only ground of inadmissibility that will likely be triggered is the controlled substance ground. However, since Marco is undocumented, he could be taken into immigration custody simply for lack of legal status. If this happens, Marco would normally be able to apply for Cancellation of Removal for Certain Non-Permanent Residents since he has been in the U.S. for over ten years and has two U.S. citizen children. But a conviction for simple possession of cocaine will make him ineligible for Cancellation, and it will also make him ineligible to get an immigration bond. Because there is no waiver available for a drug conviction (other than an offense involving thirty grams or less of marijuana), Marco will not even be able to apply for a green card when his two children turn twenty one.

Unfortunately, the consequences of a drug offense are *extremely* harsh for people who are undocumented. The best option is to plead to a non-drug offense such as disorderly conduct or resisting arrest. If you can't, you need to advise Marco that this plea will make him ineligible to get legal status in the U.S., both now and in the future. If Marco desperately wants to fight his case, consider whether there are any grounds for suppression or if he would have a good case for trial.

Remember that successful completion of some drug diversion programs will still meet the definition of a "conviction" for immigration purposes even if it is not considered a conviction for state purposes (see p. 52). Don't assume that successful completion of a drug diversion program will be "safe" for Marco.

Temporary Visa with a DUI Charge

Jeff is here legally on a valid student visa and is arrested for a simple DUI. What will be the immigration consequences if he accepts this plea?

1. **Inadmissible or Deportable?**

   Because Jeff was formally admitted to the U.S., the grounds of deportability will apply.

2. **Applicable Grounds of Removability?**

   Possibly the CIMT ground or the controlled substance ground (if the influence was drugs).

3. **Categorical Match?**

   - **CIMT:** Absent some aggravating factor that appears as an element in the statute (such as driving on a suspended license), a DUI will not be a CIMT (see p. 42-43).
   - **Controlled Substance:** If Jeff was under the influence of drugs, rather than alcohol, a conviction could conceivably trigger the controlled substance ground, though this is rare.

If Jeff's DUI involved alcohol and the statute contains no aggravating elements, this will not trigger a ground of deportability. However, the Department of Homeland Security (DHS) has broad discretion to deny entry on a visa for *any* reason, which means that Jeff could have problems if he goes home for Christmas or tries to renew his visa in the future.

You should advise Jeff that this plea will not make him deportable but it could cause problems if he travels or wants to get another visa. To be safe, Jeff should probably not leave the U.S. before he finishes his degree. Jeff should also be very responsible in complying with all his fines, classes, and other probationary requirements since this will give him the best chance to overcome the negative discretionary consequences of the DUI.

Undocumented Client with False Documents

Sara entered the U.S. illegally five years ago and has never been deported. She has aunts and uncles in the U.S., and her boyfriend is a U.S. citizen. She has no priors. Sara was arrested for using a fake social security card and charged with Fraudulent Use of Documents. She is offered a plea to a misdemeanor that has a maximum sentence of one year and can stipulate to probation.

1. **Inadmissible or Deportable?**

   Sara was not formally admitted so the grounds of inadmissibility will apply.

2. **Applicable Grounds of Removability?**

   Possibly the CIMT ground.

3. **Categorical Match?**

   CIMT: An offense that has fraud as an element will generally be considered a CIMT (see p. 39). However, a conviction will not trigger the CIMT inadmissibility ground if it is a single offense with a *potential* sentence of 365 days or less and an *actual* sentence to incarceration of 180 days or less (the "petty offense exception"). Since Sara has no priors, and since the potential sentence is 365 days and her actual sentence is zero, this conviction will not trigger inadmissibility.

Because Sara is undocumented, she could be taken into immigration custody simply for lack of lawful status. Unless she is afraid to return to her country or she has been the victim of a crime (for instance, if her boyfriend is abusive), she does not have a clear legal path to stay in the U.S. Since her conviction does not make her inadmissible, she will be eligible for an immigration bond. If she marries her boyfriend, this conviction would not disqualify her from getting legal status through him in the future, although such a process would probably have to be completed outside the U.S.

LPR with Potential Aggravated Felony

Matt came to the U.S. when he was three years old and has had a green card for 20 years. He's currently charged with receiving stolen property. Last year, he was also convicted of domestic violence and received 6 months in jail.

1. **Inadmissible or Deportable?**

   The issuance of a green card is a formal admission, so as long as Matt was not returning from abroad, the grounds of deportability will apply.

2. **Applicable Grounds of Removability?**

   Possibly a theft aggravated felony and two CIMTs for the DV and receiving stolen property convictions. Also, Matt's prior conviction may be removable by itself as a domestic violence offense.

3. Categorical Match?

- **Aggravated felony:** Yes, if he receives an actual sentence of 365 days or more.
- **Two CIMTs:** A plea to receiving stolen property will likely be a CIMT but there may be an argument against this if ICE cannot show through the record of conviction that it involved an intent to permanently, rather than temporarily deprive (see p. 42-43). The DV offense could be a CIMT but there are arguments against this if it could have lacked an intentional *mens rea,* involved *de minimus* contact, or was committed against a person with whom there was no assumption of a relationship of trust (see p. 46).
- **Domestic violence:** Matt's prior conviction may independently trigger the domestic violence ground of deportability.

You should advise Matt that, regardless of the current plea, he may already be deportable for the prior DV conviction. You should also assume conservatively that he will be removable for two CIMTs. The best thing you can do is to try to avoid an aggravated felony by negotiating a sentence of less than one year so that Matt will be eligible for Cancellation of Removal. It would also be helpful if you could plead to an intent to temporarily deprive (or leave the plea vague between temporary and permanent) in order to give Matt arguments that it's not a CIMT.

Unless there's a good argument for your state statute, you should tell Matt that if he receives a sentence of one year or more, he will be deportable for an aggravated felony and have no good way to fight his case. If you can get a sentence of less than one year, advise Matt that ICE is probably going to take him into custody and say he's deportable but that he may be able to apply for a pardon called Cancellation of Removal. Tell Matt that you're putting certain language into the plea to give him arguments that he's not deportable for a CIMT, and give him copies of the documents that show this. While he's fighting his case, Matt may be subject to mandatory detention. If he somehow manages to avoid ICE apprehension, he should NOT travel since he may be inadmissible for a CIMT upon his return.

Temporary Visa and Possession of Marijuana

Lance is a professional soccer player who travels in and out of the U.S. on a visa several times a year to compete in tournaments. After a game in Phoenix one night, he's caught with a small amount of marijuana and offered a plea to misdemeanor simple possession of marijuana.

1. **Inadmissible or Deportable?**

   Lance was admitted on a visa so the grounds of deportability apply.

2. **Applicable Grounds of Removability?**

   Controlled substance offense and a CIMT within five years of admission.

3. **Categorical Match?**

   - **Controlled substance:** The controlled substance ground of deportability contains an exception for a single offense of thirty grams or less of marijuana. Therefore, this plea will not trigger the controlled substance ground of deportability (but see below).
   - **CIMT:** Simple drug possession is not a CIMT.

This plea will not make Lance deportable. ***However, the marijuana exception for thirty grams or less does not exist in the controlled substance ground for inadmissibility***. While there is a *waiver* of inadmissibility for thirty grams or less of marijuana, it requires extreme hardship to a U.S. citizen or LPR family member, and Lance will not be eligible for it since he has no family here. Therefore, you should advise Lance that if he takes this plea, he will not be able to reenter the U.S. once he leaves. If Lance wants to continue to compete in U.S. soccer tournaments, he'll have to plead to a non-drug offense or else go to trial.

LPR with CIMT Within Five Years of Admission

Fatma entered on a visa in 2003 and got her green card on March 1, 2006. On February 1, 2011 Fatma allegedly wrote a bad check for $300. She is scheduled to enter a plea to misdemeanor Attempted Fraudulent Use of Check on April 1, 2011. While she could receive a sentence of up to one year, Fatma will almost certainly receive probation. She has no priors.

To help us keep the facts straight, let's do a quick timeline:

2003: entered U.S. on visa
March 1, 2006: got her green card
February 1, 2011: committed offense
April 1, 2011: will enter plea

1. **Inadmissible or Deportable?**

   Fatma was admitted on a visa, became an LPR, and was not apprehended at a border or airport. Therefore, the grounds of deportability will apply.

2. **Applicable Grounds of Removability?**

   Potentially a CIMT within five years of admission, an aggravated felony as fraud, and maybe an aggravated felony as forgery.

3. **Categorical Match?**

   - **CIMT:** This plea will likely be a CIMT since fraud is an element (see p. 39). It has a potential sentence of one year, so it could be a CIMT committed within five years of admission *if* March 1, 2006 was her date of admission. However, Fatma was actually admitted to the U.S. in 2003 on her visa, and the date of her green card merely reflects when she changed her status to that of an LPR. Therefore, Fatma should not have a CIMT within five years.
   - **Aggravated felony (fraud):** Although this is a fraud offense, it should not be an aggravated felony since it did not involve a loss to the victim of $10,000 or more.
   - **Aggravated felony (forgery):** The elements of this offense may meet the aggravated felony definition of forgery, but since it's unlikely she'll receive an actual sentence of incarceration of one year, this won't be an aggravated felony. However, if she violates probation and receives a year or more, this could be a problem.

You can advise Fatma that this plea should not make her deportable. However, if she travels outside the U.S., it could make her inadmissible. In theory, this conviction would meet the "petty offense exception" to inadmissibility, but it's probably better to advise Fatma not to leave the U.S. until she talks to an immigration lawyer.

Summary of important points:

- There are some common scenarios involving clients who are undocumented, who are LPRs, or who are here on a temporary visa that can be analyzed as above using the three step framework.

<u>Chapter Thirteen:</u>

PRACTICAL TIPS FOR NEGOTIATING WITH PROSECUTORS

In this chapter:

- Options to offer the prosecutor that will minimize immigration consequences
- Structuring the factual basis
- Knowing when to go to trial

One of the toughest things about representing noncitizens in criminal matters can be negotiating favorable pleas with prosecutors who are, at best, indifferent to severe immigration consequences and, at worst, zealously trying to get your client deported. Let's face it: so-called "criminal aliens" are not on everyone's party list. While there's only so much you can do to combat an unsympathetic prosecutor, here's a few suggestions for handling plea negotiations:

Figure out what the prosecutor wants.

The best way to neutralize a hostile prosecutor is to figure out what she wants and give it to her in a way that doesn't prejudice your client's immigration case. Does the prosecutor want a certain level of offense, a "strike," a particular sentence? You may not be able to give her exactly what she's looking for, but if you start by trying to understand what will satisfy her, your chances of finding a mutually acceptable plea are much greater.

Counter the plea offer with an equivalent or higher.

Most prosecutors are under political pressure to be "tough" on immigrants and would have a hard time explaining to their constituents why they gave a better deal to a noncitizen than to a citizen. When negotiating a plea for immigration purposes, try to propose an option that is an equivalent to, or higher than, the prosecutor's offer in order to calm her fear that she's giving immigrants a break.

If the only plea that will work is a lower level offense, try to offer other harsh measures as a trade-off. For instance, if you're offered a felony with probation, ask for a misdemeanor with jail time in order to fit the petty offense exception. Remind the prosecutor that, in dealing with immigrants, "different" doesn't have to mean "soft."

Don't worry about the level of the offense.

Defenders are trained to seek the lowest class of offense possible. However, apart from the exception below, the particular grade of a plea is usually irrelevant for immigration purposes. Be willing to let go of a lower class offense if it'll improve the immigration situation. For instance, the prosecutor may offer a plea to a class C felony when the particular elements of a class B felony are better for immigration purposes. It may feel disturbing to ask for a *harsher* offense, but if immigration is important to your client, don't stay so caught up in what may be a good criminal plea that you forego a good immigration plea.

The exception to this is CIMTs, which are more likely to trigger removability if there's a potential sentence of one year or more. If your client is undocumented and is pleading to his first CIMT, try to negotiate an offense that has a maximum sentence of one year (and an actual sentence of six months or less) in order to meet the "petty offense exception." If your client has been here legally for less than five years and is pleading to his first CIMT, try to negotiate an offense that has a maximum sentence of 364 days or less.

When it's helpful, be specific; when it's harmful, be vague.

This is the cardinal rule when dealing with a criminal statute that isn't a categorical match for the ground of removal. Say your client is charged with assault with a deadly weapon, and "deadly weapon" is defined in the statute as a "gun, knife, or other dangerous instrument." If your client actually had a knife, plead to "assault with a knife" in order to avoid the firearms ground. If your client actually had a gun, plead to "assault with a gun, knife, or other dangerous instrument."

Plead to an equivalent statute to get rid of bad allegations in the charging document.

One of the most damaging documents in immigration court is the charging document, e.g., the indictment, information, or complaint. Most immigration judges will assume that a person pleaded guilty to the count as it appears in the charging document and will therefore use the contents of it to determine whether the client is removable.

Sometimes it helps to plead to an alternate statute – even if the elements are similar – just to get rid of specific allegations in the charging document. For instance, in the previous example the information may allege that the assault was committed with a handgun. Instead of pleading to "assault with a deadly weapon," plead the client to "possession of a deadly weapon," which could also include a "gun, knife, or other dangerous instrument." Since the client is pleading to a different statute, the immigration judge can't consider the contents of the information and can't assume that the conviction involved a gun. In other words, pleading to a different statute – even if it's not entirely safe – can help you "cleanse" the record.

Write your own factual basis.

If the criminal statute is not a categorical match to the ground of removal, try to write your own factual basis rather than leaving it to the prosecutor. As long as it's fairly consistent with the alleged incident, many prosecutors will be less concerned about the particular language and specifics of the factual basis, thus giving you a good opportunity to create a favorable immigration plea.

Don't incorporate the police report, grand jury transcript, or other fact-based document into your plea.

One of the most damaging things for immigration cases is when the factual basis is linked to some sort of document that's loaded with bad details. When this happens, the immigration judge can assume that every detail from the police report or grand jury transcript has been incorporated into the plea and can be used to determine whether the client is removable. This is only going to be a problem when the statute is divisible and the immigration judge uses the modified categorical approach (as in the knife example above). But when in doubt, keep it out.

If you're dealing with a potential aggravated felony, plead to two counts with less than 365 days each.

If a potential ground of removal will be an aggravated felony based on the length of the sentence and you think your client might get more than one year, try pleading to two counts of 364 days, to be served consecutively. Since the immigration judge can't combine the sentences to find that your client received more than one year, the client will not have an aggravated felony. Remember that this will not work with certain aggravated felonies that don't require a one-year sentence, such as sexual abuse of a minor, drug trafficking, and fraud.

Go to trial when the immigration consequences are critical.

As with any other criminal case, the key is to figure out when the consequences of taking the plea would be as bad or worse than the consequences of losing at trial. For instance, if your undocumented client is six months away from getting his green card and is charged with possession of meth, accepting this plea will make him permanently inadmissible and lead to his deportation. Ask the client whether the consequences of losing at trial would be worse than the consequences of remaining outside of the U.S. for the rest of his life, then decide accordingly.

One advantage of going to trial is that it demonstrates to the prosecutor you're serious about immigration consequences. If the prosecutor learns that her unwillingness to negotiate could mean preparing for a trial that's not necessarily one of her priority cases, she may be more cooperative in the future.

Summary of important points:

- The most effective way to negotiate with a prosecutor is to find out what she wants and give it to her in a way that minimizes the immigration consequences. This can frequently be done by offering an equivalent or higher plea and stipulating to incarceration in exchange for an alternate plea or a particular factual basis.
- Whenever possible, avoid incorporating the police report or other documents into the factual basis, and try to write the factual basis yourself. When the facts are helpful, specifically include them in the factual basis; when the facts are harmful, track the generic language of the statute.
- Consider going to trial if all the following are true: 1) the plea will make the client removable, with little or no way to fight her immigration case; 2) the prosecutor won't negotiate; and 3) immigration status is extremely important to the client.

Chapter Fourteen

TOP TEN MISTAKES DEFENDERS MAKE WHEN ADVISING ON IMMIGRATION CONSEQUENCES

No matter how diligent you may be in researching the immigration impact of a particular plea, there are certain things about immigration law that are completely counterintuitive to the defense attorney's mindset. Here are some of the most common mistakes:

1. **"It's not a felony so it can't have immigration consequences."**

   Sometimes a defense attorney will assure me: "But this plea won't be a problem – it's a misdemeanor." This is absolutely wrong. In immigration, it's the elements of the offense, rather than whether it's a felony or a misdemeanor, that controls. While there may be exceptions for a single CIMT misdemeanor, these exceptions do NOT apply to a misdemeanor drug conviction or other non-CIMT offense, and a misdemeanor can still be an aggravated felony. In other words, never assume a plea is safe just because it's a misdemeanor.

2. **"It's not a CIMT or an aggravated felony so it can't have immigration consequences."**

   As we saw in Step Two, there are at least 14 different grounds of removability, of which CIMTs and aggravated felonies make up only two. However, since they're the most frequently discussed grounds, many defense attorneys believe that as long as it's not a CIMT or an aggravated felony, the plea will be safe. But consider: a conviction for simple possession of meth is not a CIMT or an aggravated felony, yet it will trigger both inadmissibility and deportability under the controlled substance ground. Therefore, never assume that a plea is safe just because it's not a CIMT or an aggravated felony.

3. **"It's not a conviction under state law so it can't have immigration consequences."**

   Immigration law has its own definition of "conviction," and many diversion programs will satisfy this definition even if the charges are officially dismissed and no conviction exists under state law. Look at 8 U.S.C. § 1101(a)(48)(A) to see whether your court's particular program qualifies as a "conviction" for immigration purposes. If you're unsure, assume it will .

4. **"It can't be an aggravated felony because my client didn't get a one year sentence."**

Some aggravated felonies (crime of violence, theft, burglary, and others) will only be an aggravated felony if the client receives an actual sentence of one year or more of incarceration. Others grounds of removal (drug trafficking, sexual abuse of a minor, fraud, and others) are triggered solely by the elements of the statute, regardless of the sentence imposed. Therefore, a conviction for possession for sale or molestation of a child will likely be an aggravated felony no matter what sentence the client receives.

Also, a sentence of incarceration that results from a probation violation will be considered part of the final sentence. So remember that a probation violation could turn a non-aggravated felony into an aggravated felony.

5. **"Possession of paraphernalia is a safe plea."**

Possession of drug paraphernalia triggers both inadmissibility and deportability as a controlled substance offense and will usually have the same consequences as a conviction for simple drug possession. A waiver of inadmissibility (but not deportability) *may* be available if the paraphernalia related to a single offense of thirty grams or less of marijuana for one's own personal use.

6. **"My client is undocumented but is applying for citizenship."**

This is a common statement by defense attorneys that can lead to misunderstandings with immigration attorneys. A person can go from being undocumented, to being an LPR, to being a naturalized U.S. citizen, but a person can never go directly from undocumented to naturalized U.S. citizen. Therefore, when a defender says, "the client is applying for citizenship," an immigration attorney may mistakenly believe that the client is an LPR and give inaccurate advice. Remember: a client who is undocumented is never applying for citizenship – she's applying for LPR status.

7. **"My client came in 2000 and has her green card so it can't be a CIMT within five years of admission."**

If a client entered illegally and later received her green card, her official date of admission is the date she got her green card, *not* when she physically entered. Many defenders tell me, "Oh, the client's been here forever" and later find out that the client only became an LPR two years ago. Especially when considering whether the client is deportable for a CIMT within five years of admission, make sure you calculate from the date she was formally admitted on a visa or as an LPR – *not* when she illegally entered.

8. "I don't need to ask about priors since I can't do anything about them."

It's true that you can't do much about prior offenses, particularly if your client is already removable as a result of them. But sometimes the immigration consequences of the *current* plea are also dependent on the client's priors; for instance, an LPR who accepts a plea to simple possession of thirty grams or less of marijuana will be removable if she has a prior marijuana conviction since the thirty gram or less exception only applies to a "single" offense. Remember to specifically inquire about misdemeanors and any diversion programs since many clients may not consider these "convictions."

9. "The date of conviction, rather than the date of commission, controls."

In calculating removability and eligibility for relief, the date that the alleged offense was committed can be critical. The most important example of this involves removability for a CIMT that is committed within five years of admission; thus, a client who is admitted in 2005, commits a CIMT in 2009, and is convicted in 2011 will be removable. A client's ability to fight her case may also depend on whether the date of commission "cut" the time necessary to apply for a waiver or pardon.

10. "I advised my client on the immigration consequences but he's still filing a complaint against me!"

Many immigrants are desperate to be reunited with their families and will use any legal hook available to obtain or reclaim legal status. If you work with a high number of noncitizens, it's inevitable that a former client will come after you sooner or later, whether or not your advice was correct. When this happens, take an honest look at whether you provided accurate information, get a second opinion, and be willing to fall on your sword if you made a mistake. Your best defense against ineffective claims is to double-check your advice and keep good records. But don't take it personally if a *Padilla* claim is filed against you; it's just the nature of the work.

GLOSSARY

ABC Class Membership: *American Baptist Churches v. Thornburgh* (commonly referred to as "ABC," or the "ABC lawsuit") was filed in 1985 and alleged discriminatory treatment against Guatemalans and Salvadorans who had applied for asylum. The ABC settlement provides certain protections relating to detention, asylum, and other issues for class members.

Adjustment of Status: The process of acquiring lawful permanent residence while inside the U.S., usually through the I-130 petition of a relative or following a grant of asylum or refugee status.

Aggravated Felony: A ground of deportability and the most serious type of immigration offense. An aggravated felony makes a noncitizen ineligible for most forms of relief, and a person who is deported with an aggravated felony is barred from future legal status. An aggravated felon who illegally reenters the U.S. after deportation is also subject to serious enhancements under the U.S. Sentencing Guidelines.

Amnesty: Usually refers to the Immigration Reform and Control Act of 1986, which provided temporary legal status to people present in the U.S. before January 1, 1982 and certain seasonal agricultural workers. Most people who received "amnesty" went on to get LPR status, though not all did.

Asylum: A form of relief for people who can show past persecution or a well-founded fear of persecution on account of their race, religion, nationality, political opinion, or membership in a particular social group.

Board of Immigration Appeals (BIA): The immigration administrative appeals court that creates much of the case law for determining immigration consequences of convictions.

Border Crossing Card (BCC): Also known as a visitor's visa, a B1/B2, or a "laser visa," a BCC is usually valid for ten years and allows the holder to enter for a maximum of six months.

Cancellation of Removal for LPRs: Allows an LPR who is removable to request a one-time "pardon." Judge will weigh the equities to decide whether relief is merited.

Cancellation of Removal for Non-LPRs: A form of relief for undocumented noncitizens who have been in U.S. for ten years and whose removal would cause "exceptional and extremely unusual hardship" to a U.S. citizen or LPR spouse, child, or parent.

Categorical Approach: A method of determining whether the elements of a state, local, or federal statute match the elements of an immigration statute such that the conviction will trigger a ground of removal.

Convention Against Torture (CAT): A treaty-based form of relief that forbids removal to a country where the person will be tortured or killed.

Crime Involving Moral Turpitude (CIMT): A ground of inadmissibility and deportability covering offenses that are "inherently base, vile, or depraved," "reprehensible," *malum in se*, or conduct that violates norms and shocks the public conscience.

Department of Homeland Security (DHS): The government agency that encompasses the three primary immigration agencies: Customs and Border Protection (CBP), Immigration and Customs Enforcement (ICE), and U.S. Citizenship and Immigration Services (USCIS). Generally, CBP controls the borders, ICE controls interior enforcement and removal, and USCIS controls applications for benefits, such as work permits and naturalization.

Deportable: An offense that makes a client who has been lawfully admitted to the U.S. subject to deportation. Along with "inadmissible," one of two subsets of "removable."

Employment Authorization Document (EAD): A "work permit" that allows the holder to legally work in the U.S. An EAD is not, by itself, a form of legal status and does not confer legal status.

"Green card": A common term for lawful permanent residence, or "LPR" status.

I-94: An Arrival-Departure Record that temporary immigrants are required to complete when they enter the U.S. An I-94 is not a legal status by itself, but it reflects that someone has entered legally, usually on a visa or as a refugee.

I-130: A petition submitted by a spouse, parent, sibling, or adult son or daughter who is a U.S. citizen or LPR to request lawful permanent residence for a relative.

I-551: A "green card," or the "resident alien" card reflecting that a person is a lawful permanent resident.

Immigration and Customs Enforcement (ICE): The enforcement and removal branch of the Department of Homeland Security. The agency that used to be known as the "INS."

Inadmissible: An offense that makes a client who has not been lawfully admitted to the U.S. ineligible to get legal status in the future. Along with "deportable," one of two subsets of "removable."

Laser Visa: Also known as a Border Crossing Card. Laser visas issued prior to October 1, 2008 are still valid for entry until their expiration date, which is usually ten years.

Lawful Permanent Resident (LPR): Also known as a "green card holder," lawful permanent residence allows a noncitizen to live and work permanently in the U.S.

Modified Categorical Approach: The approach used to determine removability when parts of the statute of conviction reach conduct that would be removable and parts do not. The modified categorical approach allows the immigration adjudicator to consult the formal record of conviction, including the charging document, judgment, plea colloquy, jury instructions, and any factual basis to which the defendant assented in order to determine whether the conduct for which the defendant was convicted is removable. *See Taylor v. U.S.,* 495 U.S. 575 (1990).

NACARA: The Nicaraguan Adjustment and Central American Relief Act. Under NACARA, a person who came from a certain country and/or applied for asylum before a certain date may be a member of a class or eligible to get legal status on that basis alone. This applies to citizens of Guatemala, El Salvador, Nicaragua, Cuba, and countries from the former Soviet bloc.

Parole: A grant of discretionary permission to enter the U.S., often for certain compelling humanitarian reasons, or to serve as a material witness or undergo criminal prosecution. A person "paroled" into the U.S., is legally treated as though he is still at the border even though he has been allowed to physically enter the U.S.

Petition (often known as an I-130): An application submitted by a spouse, parent, sibling, or adult son or daughter who is a U.S. citizen or LPR to request lawful permanent residence for a relative.

Petty Offense Exception: An exception to inadmissibility for a single CIMT with a *potential* sentence of 365 days or less and an *actual* sentence of 180 days or less.

Refugee: A person who was determined to meet the requirements for asylum while outside the U.S., most likely by the United Nations High Commissioner for Refugees.

Removal Proceedings: The process of being legally expelled from the country through a series of administrative hearings.

Removable: A person who can be removed from the U.S., usually due to lack of lawful status, an immigration violation, criminal conduct, or a psychological or physical condition.

S Visa: A visa for individuals who possess critical, reliable information about a terrorist group or criminal enterprise and are willing to cooperate with government officials. Commonly known as a "Snitch visa."

Special Agricultural Workers (SAW): In 1986, the Immigration Control and Reform Act allowed certain undocumented seasonal agricultural laborers to apply for amnesty and ultimately receive permanent residence.

Special Immigrant Juvenile Status: Provides LPR status to minors who have been declared dependent on the state and are eligible for long-term foster care.

Supervised Release: A type of release for noncitizens who have been ordered removed but cannot be physically returned to their country of origin, usually due to the absence of a repatriation agreement.

T Visa: A form of relief for a trafficking victim who has suffered substantial physical or mental abuse and has been, is, or is willing to be helpful in investigation or prosecution.

Temporary Protected Status (TPS): A temporary permission to stay in the U.S. for citizens of certain countries that suffer from armed conflict or a natural disaster, during which they may receive work authorization. The most recent countries that have been designated for TPS are El Salvador, Haiti, Honduras, Nicaragua, Somalia, and Sudan.

U Visa: A form of relief for a victim of crime who has suffered substantial physical or mental abuse and has been, is, or is willing to be helpful in investigation or prosecution.

Violence Against Women Act (VAWA): A form of relief that allows victims of domestic violence to petition for legal status in the United States without relying on an abusive U.S. citizen or LPR spouse, parent, or child to sponsor them.

Visa: Formal permission to enter the U.S. on a temporary basis as a visitor, student, entertainer, etc.

Voluntary Departure: A form of relief that allows a noncitizen to leave without an official order of deportation, which may make it easier to come back in the future if a legal route exists to do so.

Withholding of Removal: A form of protection similar to asylum that's more difficult to get and only ensures that the person will not be sent to a particular country. No possibility of permanent residence or bringing family to U.S.

INDEX